WAVELENGTHS

Joe Ziemer

authorHOUSE·

AuthorHouse™
1663 Liberty Drive
Bloomington, IN 47403
www.authorhouse.com
Phone: 833-262-8899

Published by AuthorHouse 12/15/2022

ISBN: 978-1-6655-7855-4 (hc)

Print information available on the last page.

Scripture quotations marked NIV are taken from the Holy Bible, New International Version®. NIV®. Copyright © 1973, 1978, 1984 by International Bible Society. Used by permission of Zondervan. All rights reserved. [Biblica]

This book is printed on acid-free paper.

For my children –

Donovan, Jamie, Kris, Joey and Megan

TABLE OF CONTENTS

Preface   5

Foreword by Martin Hall   6

EXPLORATION

Heaven on Earth: The Venezuela That Was   9
Heaven on Earth: The Venezuela That Was *(in Spanish)*   109

The Riverside Cadet: Life in a Military Academy   27

Shady Lady of Shady Lane   49

Be All You Can Be   57

EXCURSION

The Train   65

The Beatles   67

Sitting Backwards on a Train   69

Anam Cara   73

Haikus with a Twist   74

I Would Give It All   76

There She Stood / You Here Me There   77

The Little College That Could   79

Sad Eyed Lady   80

Briefcase Blues   81

Anchors Aweigh   83

Lucille / Juliet's Prayer   84

Low-Level Wavelength   85

The Stone   86

IMMERSION

Crystal & Stone - New Intro to the 2nd Edition 88

Ron 92

A Day with The Mick 95

Maggie the Bohemian 100

A Wavelength Thing 106

About the Illustrator 128

About the Author 129

The front cover design and all illustrations in <u>Wavelengths</u> were created by Brandon Olterman.

PREFACE

Why title a book <u>Wavelengths</u>? The word refers to sound or electronic waves, such as radio waves. It also means a person's ideas and way of thinking, especially as it affects an ability to connect with others. This second meaning, a social-psychological view, is the common fabric of pieces in this book.

According to a 2018 study by UCLA and Dartsmouth researchers, friends are "cognitively homophilous," meaning they share similar neural brain patterns. In layman's terms, the brains of friends respond in remarkably parallel ways, literally meaning friends are on the same wavelength.

Aristotle advanced this basic notion over 2,300 years ago, writing, "Love is composed of a single soul inhabiting two bodies." I believe Aristotle was philosophizing about the relationship referred to today as "soulmate." On the amity scale, soulmates are at the pinnacle. They can sometimes read each other's mind, in my experience, and think the same thought at the same time. I believe this is a karmic, if not spiritual, bond.

Whatever wavelength we have is a gift from God, as He has all the bandwidth. I believe this is how God hears prayer. I also believe, as the <u>Bible</u> teaches, that if we sincerely acknowledge Him in all our ways and with all our hearts, we can hear Him, too. His love for all of mankind, or agape (selfless) love, is a supreme passion that we can, at best, only try to imagine. This is a book about the best kind of human love... be it eros (romantic)... storge (familial)... or philia (brotherly)... the kind of love that comes from being on the same wavelength as another soul.

<u>Wavelengths</u> is divided into three sections. The first part, **Exploration,** consists of four essays, all dealing with love: love for the Venezuela that was, for an alma mater, for God and for Mom. **Excursion** is made up of bursts of love for trains, friends, a child, a woman and above all, God. Excursion also has my takes on Vegas, boating, briefcases, Butler, Beatles and Joan Baez. The final section, **Immersion**, is comprised of five articles about a brilliant singer-songwriter, a unique human being and a friend, Mickey Newbury.

Mark Twain wrote, "Writing is easy. All you have to do is cross out the wrong words." While Twain was being somewhat modest, I hope I have crossed out most of the wrong words, and I hope you enjoy <u>Wavelengths</u>.

FOREWORD
BY MARTIN HALL

You are about to join Joe Ziemer on a journey through his life. He explains in the Preface his choice of Wavelengths for the title to this book. But I invite you to consider that wavelength in electronics is often displayed graphically as the measure of a signal from peak to peak, with a trough (low peak) in between adjoining high peaks. It is appropriate, then, as you read Wavelengths, that Joe will share with you some of his peak moments and experiences, and he will also share with you some of his unvarnished trough, low experiences. You will get the full measure of the man; you will get the wavelength of Joe.

You will come to see one of the amazing things about Joe is his balance of being highly technical and organized, while at the same time being fully present and connected artistically and emotionally. Balance of that sort at his level of accomplishment is rare, especially as he has been a prolific writer and producer of all manner of works. There are many pleasant surprises about Joe waiting for you on your Wavelengths journey.

It is pleasing for those of us who know Joe to at last be able to get to know more of his back story. If you do not already know Joe, you will know him by the facts which define him, but, more important, you will know him by his heart, by his family, by his faith, and by his commitment to doing the right thing for the right reason with love. That is Joe Ziemer.

It was Joe's selfless devotion and commitment to the life and work of Mickey Newbury that drew us together well over two decades ago. You need look no further than Joe's Crystal and Stone volumes about Mickey to gauge Joe's loving persistence in crossing meaningful finish lines with grace. More than anyone in Mickey's world, Joe has documented the considerable substance of Mickey's professional life. But that is only one measure of who Joe is.

The rest of the story is where Joe begins sharing his journey with us here, with his opening lines of Wavelengths. Enjoy...

~~~~~~

EXPLORATION

Deep dives into Venezuela, a military academy
and my sweet Lord. Mom, too.

The "Lighthouse of Maracaibo" over the 5.4-mile Gen. Rafael Urdaneta Bridge

HEAVEN ON EARTH:
THE VENEZUELA THAT WAS

(This article appears in Spanish on page 109.)

Like real-life characters drawn from a John Steinbeck novel, my parents left Oklahoma after the Second World War. With all of their possessions tied to the top of a 1938 Plymouth, Kelly and LaWanda joined the wave of emigration from the poor land to the Promised Land. Along with thousands of Okies, they traveled 1,800 miles on Route 66, looking for jobs, dignity and a future. They went west on the Mother Road, all the way to the end of the line, to the Golden Land of California.

I was born in 1948 and spent my boyhood years in sunbaked Bakersfield, a rich oil and agricultural town, populated by dreamers and roughnecks, where fighting was an accepted way of making friends. Though the area's temperature was hot as hell, I have cool memories of riding the Kern River, well before whitewater rafting became a sport.

When I turned 12, Dad moved the family south... to an even hotter area in the steamy tropics... to an even richer oil town... to Maracaibo, Venezuela, magical land of sloths, river dolphins, Orinoco crocodiles and giant anteaters. A land where my sister and I felt like we were the only blondes in the country.

Venezuela has been an oil producer for 100 years, and with 300 billion barrels has the largest oil cache of any nation. Dad went there in 1961 hoping to earn his fortune as a platform worker for Standard Oil of California (Chevron). From offshore drilling on a mighty lake to the rigors of the Boscán bush land, the work was exhausting and dangerous. With five days on and five days off, drillers needed to keep one eye on an overhead crane and one eye out for colorful, creepy creatures.

Truly, the South American nation has been blessed with stunning landscapes. On his third voyage to the Americas in 1497, Columbus sailed to the mouth of Venezuela's Orinoco River and declared he had found "Heaven on Earth." Nicknamed "Little Venice" by Spanish explorers - after observing houses on stilts over water - Venezuela is indeed a heavenly land. Its diverse beauty ranges from magnificent 15,000 foot Andes mountain peaks (in the west)... to the otherworldly Amazon rainforest (south)... to 1,700 miles of majestic Caribbean coast (north)... to the mighty Orinoco River (east).

Though Venezuela is in dire straits today due to corruption of selfish tyrants, it was a vivacious, economic powerhouse in the sixties and seventies, when all essential pieces came together. Upon departing authoritarian rule in 1961, their constitution was modelled after the US constitution. Next, the monetary currency, Bolívar, was fixed to the US dollar at an exchange rate of 4.3 to 1.

Add in a stable government, massive oil production plus gold and diamonds, and the country was on its merry way to the most prosperous era in its history. One tell-tale sign: hands down, Venezuela had the largest middle class in all of Latin America. Scotch whiskey consumption was the highest in the world; the middle class drove Fords and Volkswagens and jetted off on shopping sprees to Miami, where they were known as "dame dos" (give me two.)

So, we arrived in the summer of 1961 just when all this change was starting. Dad had arranged our 22-hour flight to Maracaibo via the Pan Am turbo-prop route: L.A. to Mexico to Guatemala to Panama to Colombia to Venezuela. Somewhere over Colombia, we hit sudden, deadly turbulence, causing the plane to go into a steep dive and slow spin. Everybody was screaming, except Mom, who said, "Joe, tighten Paulette's seat belt!"

After what seemed an eternity, the pilot pulled the nose up and we recovered. Mom laughed out loud that the man sitting behind us had upchucked all over our new traveling clothes. When we landed, medics boarded the craft and carried the pilot out on a stretcher. He had hurt his back while maneuvering the airplane. What did we learn on this day? First, in an airplane going down, there are no atheists. And second, there is not a damn thing wrong with kissing the ground.

While kissing the tarmac, the first thing I noticed was the heat. Hit me like a freight train. Located 10 degrees north of the equator and 70 miles south of the Caribbean, Maracaibo is HOT. We arrived in June with 95-degree temperature and 70% humidity, which "feels like" 124 degrees.

In the customs area, we entered a slow queue leading to uniformed men behind long tables. When our turn came some three hours later, the angriest looking one began our inspection by asking, "Do you have anything you wish to declare?" "Not now," answered I in my best Honest Abe impersonation. Mom bit her lip as the annoyed agent began digging through our suitcases. In retrospect, he was not angry, just hot. And he was not impressed with a wise-ass, 12-year-old Gringo. A pale-face who stood all of 4 feet, 11 inches.

As we exited customs, Dad was there waiting and quickly had us in a car with the undisputed luxury of third-world tropics... air conditioning. During the 30-minute drive to our apartment, it struck me that everybody in this city was Venezuelan, a thought that was simultaneously fascinating and terrifying. And they were all speaking Spanish. I was, for the first time, in a minority.

Still, there is something quite magical about starting fresh in another country, that is, to be taken out of one's comfort zone and whisked away to a totally different environment. Not simply the turn of a page to a new chapter, but a whole new story. With new friends. New foods. And a new language.

We were ecstatic to be in our apartment. Located on Calle 67 between Avenidas 3D and 3E, the three-story building, Edificio Don Carlos, looked out over picturesque Lake Maracaibo, the largest lake in all of South America. At 28 million years old and fed by over 135 rivers, it is the third oldest lake in the world. It is also the most active area for lightning strikes on the planet. Commonly called Catatumbo lightning, during major storms, the "Lighthouse of Maracaibo" frequently produces more than 40 lightning strikes per minute. From our apartment balcony, we often enjoyed God's astonishing light show. An all-night-long explosion of jagged white light from the heavens.

On our first morning in the apartment, I thought Mom was playing charades with the maid, Selena. (Everybody in Venezuela has a maid.) With wild hand motions, Mom was doing her best to "ask" her to make oatmeal for breakfast. My sister Paulette and I saw Selena nod as she began boiling water. A few minutes later, she served us a bowl of hot broth. Selena had strained the cooked oatmeal and served us the juice. "Gracias," Mom said to Selena. "Drink it," said Mom to her kids.

After breakfast, I walked down the stairs to the outside of our apartment. There, I saw a boy a bit older than myself, who appeared to be Venezuelan. We both said hello, and I asked him if he would like to play a little football. Yes, he answered, and we both ran upstairs to our apartments. He returned with a round, black-and-white ball, and I came back with an American football. One of my first lessons: the word for soccer in Spanish is "fútbol."

The boy that I met in June of 1961 has been my best friend to this very day. Augusto Socarrás is actually Colombian, and his family lived on the third story of our building, while we lived one flight below. He had two younger brothers...

Chemi age six and Cuchi - four, plus three younger sisters, Carolina - nine, Clemencia - eight and Elizabeth - one. Augusto's dad, Luis Napoleón Ferreira ("Napo"), was a brilliant architect; and his mother, Ligia, became a second mother to me. Almost instantly.

Sometimes in life, in the most unexpected places and under the strangest set of circumstances, we meet someone who is tuned to our exact wavelength. The occasion is a rarity and a blessing. Augusto took me under his wing, and he showed me the ropes. I was a stranger on foreign soil, and he made me feel welcomed. On my first day in another land, I did not feel alone.

One of the first things Augusto taught me was how to say the dirty words in Spanish. They remain a steadfast preference over their English counterparts. Cursing in Spanish just sounds so much more romantic, as well as emphatic. An indoctrination to Venezuelan vernacular would not be complete, however, without a few additional key words. A person from Maracaibo is a Maracucho, and when he wishes to say fantastic or cool, he would simply say "chévere." And if a Maracucho is asked how he is doing, he might answer, "machete," which means great.

Before we left California, I had studied Spanish in the 7th grade, and that one year of instruction did help a bit. But my sister Paulette became playmates with Augusto's brothers and sisters, mainly Cuchi, who was her same age. At four years of age, she was completely immersed in the Spanish language, in a fun way, and within about six months, she was fluent. In short order, Paulette became the family diplomat, especially when we wanted oatmeal.

Our family was submerged in Latin culture, and I loved it. If the paintings of Norman Rockwell present the idyllic family on canvas, then Augusto's people, the Ferreira's, could have been the models. I mean, his family was so loving. And respectful. And humble. And rock-solid sane.

They embodied the best of Latin culture and family values. Their priorities were God, family, work and play - in that order. "All for one and one for all" was their unspoken motto, and they held to that standard every single day. After being "adopted" by the Ferreira's, my Ugly American slant was levelled.

Once my head was on straight, I had a blast during my first year in Venezuela. Climbing 40-foot coconut trees. Enjoying the pristine beach of La Cañada, a peaceful village near Maracaibo, where people and waves rolled slowly.

Catching green iguanas that grow up to five feet long and weigh 20 pounds. Sleeping in a colorful "chinchorro," a hammock weaved by Guajiros Indians. Strumming the Venezuelan cuatro, a four-string instrument that sounds like a lovely cross between a mandolin and a 12-string guitar.

My favorite activity was swimming in the clean, crystal-clear, 87-degree water of Lake Maracaibo, a regenerative experience that made me feel "reborn." And we must include cooking a whole pig in the ground, Venezuelan style. Few tastes in this world compare to the first bite of pork that has just fallen off the bones of a pig you spent two days roasting and smelling, which brings us to the local cuisine. Influenced by the romantic cultures of Europe and indigenous traditions, Venezuelan fare is delicious beyond words.

The discussion must start with arepas, a cornerstone of the Venezuelan diet. Made from corn dough and about half an inch thick, arepas are fried or grilled and typically filled with butter and white cheese. Ingredients can include beef, chicken, pork, black beans, avocado and eggs. Arepa stands stood on street corners all over Maracaibo, where for only two Bolivars (about 45 US cents), you could buy a scrumptious arepa filled with whatever your heart desired. After late-night teen parties, Augusto and I could be found at our beloved arepa stand on Bella Vista street.

At the teen parties, where we grooved to Chubby Checker's twist in this era, the host would serve tequeños, a fried wheat flour with white cheese inside. A plate of eight of them were sold at most clubs and on street corners for one Bolivar. The host might also serve empanadas, a corn flour snack containing white cheese or shredded beef. At Christmas time, we would enjoy hallacas, a steamed mixture of beef, pork, chicken, capers, raisins and olives wrapped in cornmeal and bound with string within plantain leaves. And while walking anywhere, mouthwatering mangos were at our beck and call. We would just reach up and pluck them from the trees.

If we were hot and thirsty, often the case in Maracaibo, we would look out for a donkey or bicycle-drawn cart peddling cepillaos. The vendor would scrape a large block of ice with a stiff brush to collect "snow ice" to fill a plastic cup. We would choose from natural flavors, such as mint, coca, guava, mango, lemon, banana, coconut and pineapple. As a grand finale, the vendor would top off the flavor with a sweet, heavy cream. The price for this heavenly concoction? One medio (25 Venezuelan cents) or one American nickel.

In addition to cepillaos, several satisfying thirst-quenchers were available. Delicious, natural fruit drinks were sold everywhere. Coca Cola had its own bottling plant in Maracaibo. Locally brewed beers included Zulia and Polar, both containing 5% alcohol. Venezuelan dark rum was particularly popular, and Ron Anejo was the preferred brand. It was a smooth blend of several rums aged for a minimum period of two years in white oak casks. Though I tasted of the forbidden fruit, I was really too young to partake.

For just half the price of a cepillao (one locha), street vendors carrying large silver thermoses peddled espressos well before the existence of Starbucks. Sourced from locally grown beans, the strong coffee was served hot, black and super sweet. A pick-me-up in a Dixie cup, this satisfying single shot was the ultimate jolt of energy.

I recall one day when I was broke and wanted an espresso. As necessity is the mother of invention, I devised a strategy to obtain a coffee gratis. Speaking with a kind street vendor, I entered my first commercial negotiation.

"Hola, amigo," said I to the vendor. "How is your coffee today?"
"It is good, señor."
"I know it is. As a loyal customer, I always try to get my coffee here."
"Gracias, señor," said the vendor appreciatively.
"But today I am sad because I cannot buy your coffee."
"Why not, señor?"
"I cannot enjoy your coffee because today I am without money."
"Ay, señor, I am sorry."
"I am sorry also, because I know you want to see your customers happy."
"Si, señor, that is correct."
"As a happy customer, I come here many times because I love your coffee."
"Gracias, señor," said the vendor appreciatively.
"And of course, you know that I will come again to enjoy your coffee?"
"Si, señor, I hope so," said the vendor in a lower tone.
"But today I wish I was happy."
"Ay, señor, it is only coffee," said the vendor as he looked away.
"Yes, but it lifts me up, and then I can be on my way."
"Okay, señor, I will treat you to one cafecito, and then I will see you tomorrow."

The coffee poured for me that day by the kind vendor was a jolt of satisfaction. The basic training was important because most goods in Venezuela were negotiable. An exception was in the super stores, where prices were fixed.

Maracaibo had the first supermarkets in Venezuela, a chain called "Todos" ("everything" in Spanish) that was owned by the prominent Rockefeller family. The city also had a Sears department store, located on 5 de Julio avenue. Todos and Sears were trendy shopping spots for locals, due to the extensive selection of quality goods, competitive pricing and yes, air conditioning.

But cleanliness, convenience and climate control were no match for the thrill of Old Town shopping. There were Cuban cigars and original oil paintings. Pet monkeys and 18-karat gold chains. Record players and alligator shoes. The smell of arepas and coffee mixed with bus fumes and sweaty animals.

Located at the bottom of Maracaibo close to colorful, historic, colonial houses, Old Town is the original downtown. Most anything could be negotiated there, including, I am sure, contraband, dance partners and mind-bending potions. Though our family shopped in Old Town for fruit, vegetables and fresh fish, we never knew what we might see, hear or smell. There were traditional store fronts and vendors in the street. There were runners who could find anything, sell anything. Señor, would you like to see a blue and gold parrot?

Our family went down to Old Town many times to shop, visit the post office and catch the ferry. In 1961, Dad often ferried across Lake Maracaibo to the booming city of Cabimas, a center of oil production, or to the Boscán oil field. To catch the auto ferry ("la flecha") from the old pier at Calle 100, we would be in the car line at 4:00 AM. With luck, we would be on our way by 7:00 AM, just before the sun began cooking the city. Waiting in line, we were always entertained by the unending parade of insistent street vendors at our window, hawking everything from belts to bullets to batteries.

In August of 1962, the ferry went the way of the buggy whip when the General Rafael Urdaneta Bridge opened, connecting Maracaibo to Cabimas and eastern Venezuela. This marvel of construction took five years to complete, and at 5.4 miles long, is seven times the length of the Golden Gate Bridge.

Not only did we enjoy a perfect view of the bridge from our apartment balcony, but the new bridge saved Dad 10 hours per week. For his physical well-being, that was a big deal. The poor guy would arrive home filthy and dead tired from laboring on a hot Boscán oil derrick or on an off-shore drilling platform. With a brutal schedule of five straight days on, the man needed to recuperate. But Kelly Ziemer was proud to be an Okie-Bakersfield working man, and yes, he liked the music of Merle Haggard. Ray Charles, too.

Dad was very well compensated for the hard work, and after about six months, our family had accumulated a bit of a nest egg. My folks began saving money to purchase a house, plus we could afford to eat out occasionally.

The street food in Maracaibo was delicious, and the restaurants were sublime. My favorite restaurant in the world was (and still is) located at the corner of Avenida 3H and Calle 76. "Mi Vaquita" ("my little cow") opened its doors about six months after we arrived in country. We would order the mixed grill, and while the menu stated it would serve up to two people, Dad and I would each order our own. The waiter would roll out a little barbeque pit to tableside. Sizzling on the grill were several choice cuts of seasoned meat, including lamb chops, beef liver, chicken breast, chorizo sausage and six-ounce filets. The juicy steak came from 100% grass-fed stock, and the sweet aroma of that magnificent serving lives in my memory to this day.

Another popular eatery frequented by the Ziemers was located at Avenida 23, between Calles 66 and 67. Much less expensive than the exalted Mi Vaquita, the Rincon Boricua restaurant was a favorite of the children. With go-carts, carnival games and a large outdoor screen featuring cartoons and movies, Rincon served the best broasted chicken-in-a-basket that I have ever tasted. Served with yucca and fries, this dinner delight was available for only 8 Bs. So, for $1.85 US, we would sit outside at picnic tables, in the evening when the hot sun was down and the evening was cool, devouring crunchy chicken and enjoying the latest "Three Stooges" movie.

As the cost of local gasoline was very cheap, transportation around the city was ridiculously inexpensive. Public busses cost one medio (25 Venezuelan cents or just one American nickel), but they were usually packed with people. If standing room only was not your preference, then "carritos" were available; these passenger cars (Fords, Chevrolets, whatever) followed a specific route. A person would wait for a carrito (like waiting for a bus), and the driver would deliver him anywhere along the designated route. Perfectly safe and clean, carritos ran all day and most of the night. Cost to go most places by carrito? One real or 50 Venezuelan cents (12 US cents).

Augusto and I took carritos all the time, and we never experienced a problem. The streets of Maracaibo were safe and peaceful, never a threat of danger. Maracuchos were friendly, fun-loving and regardless of their station in life, most locals would immediately go out of their way to assist a person in need.

A person by himself would not walk down a dark alley in Old Town at 3 AM, waving one-hundred-dollar bills in the air. But the point is that Augusto and I never experienced a crisis, never felt vulnerable on the Maracaibo streets.

Before we would head out to the bright lights, Augusto's mom would bless us, saying "bendición," as she made the sign of the cross in the air. Her blessing made us feel like we were wearing invisible shields. Feeling secure and with great anticipation of a fun evening, Augusto and I would party on Saturday with our friends, but on Sunday, we often went to church.

Where would we go in a carrito? To athletic clubs. To movies. To visit friends. We spent hours and hours in the athletic clubs, swimming, eating tequeños and checking out the beautiful girls. "Beautiful girls" is not just an opinion. Venezuela has taken eight Miss International titles, seven Miss Universe titles, six Miss World titles and two Miss Earth titles, making it the only country to win all four pageants multiple times. The gorgeous Venezuelan girls were everywhere it seemed, especially at the clubs, and they were so friendly.

Most clubs had Olympic-size swimming pools, tennis courts and dining areas. Club Creole and Club Bella Vista were our favorites, but we also enjoyed Club Alianza, Club Náutico, Club Comercio and of course, the ritzy Hotel Del Lago. The clubs would host weekend parties, but Augusto and I could not afford to join every club in town. And so, we always found some way to be invited. What did we do at these parties? We danced.

The music was alive. Like some kind of mythical creature, it would grab us and tell our feet what to do. The Pied Piper of Dance, the gaita Zuliana, is a dance music that originated in Maracaibo in the 60's. In its most primal form, singers are accompanied by basic folk instruments, including the furro drum, cuatro, maracas, tambora and charrasca. Venezuelan musicians infused the traditional gaita with a hot shot of salsa and a sweet measure of merengue, adding conga and trumpet and bass guitar, and exaggerated hip movements were unleashed. Joyful Venezuelans moving on the jam-packed dance floor were a supremely confident and composed presence in the eternal groove. This was, after all, their music. Their party. Their celebration of life.

They had so much to celebrate, for starters, camaraderie of the people. Even with strangers, the friendliness was exceptional and something I had not experienced. They were also blessed to live in one of the most beautiful environments on the planet with spectacular beaches, mountains and jungles.

Additionally, as they were enjoying the uppermost median income in all of Latin America, their standard of living had rocketed to its highest level ever. In other words, they could afford to purchase good food, a car, a vacation. Finally, the government was making major improvements in the infrastructure by constructing new schools, new hospitals, new highways and new bridges. Whichever direction one looked, the nation was making life-altering changes. And so, the people danced.

But we did not dance all the time. Just as Dad had work to do, we had school to attend. Paulette and I rode a bus a short distance to an American school, Escuela Bella Vista. It was a small school that offered standard subjects, and I played a few sports. My favorite class was "Playing the Cuatro."

Augusto attended a Catholic high school, San Vicente de Paul, also a short distance from home. His school, along with most Venezuelan high schools, required completion of five years of difficult curriculum, with strong subjects, such as physics and calculus and mandatory foreign language immersion. Before final exams, Venezuelan students would stay up all night studying. During this era, I believe the typical Venezuelan **high-school** graduate would have tested out as more literate than the typical American **college** graduate.

With tremendous investment in education by a stable government, by 1965, approximately 90% of the population was literate. The public University of Zulia in Maracaibo would become one of the leading universities in the world, offering professional degrees in law, medicine, engineering. The country was producing an intelligent and competent work force to carry the nation forward. Not only were Venezuelan girls pretty and friendly. They were smart, too.

As the 1962-63 school year drew near, my parents decided that I should attend Riverside Military Academy in Georgia. Dad's friend, Blackie Armel, who lived across the street from us, had a son, Steve, who was a senior at the all-boys school. And so, in September of 1962, I entered the academy and would remain there for four years of high school.

But I returned to Maracaibo for summers. By this time, Dad had formed a partnership with Frank Bernard, an upright and loyal colleague from Trinidad. In 1963, they incorporated a start-up firm called "Tri-Can," a supplier to the local oil industry of directional-drilling expertise and supplies.

Business was good for Dad, and it would get better. He had been in country long enough by then to establish a name for himself and dependable contacts. The man worked very hard, day and night, and he earned what he received. We had moved a short distance to a new high-rise, to Edificio Yonekura, at Bella Vista and Calle 83. The new apartment was modern and spacious, and I hosted a few teen parties there. We drank cokes and danced to the timeless music of Roy Orbison, Bobby Solo and The Beach Boys.

During that summer, I met a sweet girl, Irma, who became my first girlfriend. Irma's family was from Mexico, and her dad was working a job in Maracaibo. She did not speak English at all, and my Spanish at the time was hit and miss, so whenever we were together, we kept a Spanish/English dictionary at hand. If I were to ask Irma if she would like to go to a movie or to visit a friend... we would look up the question, *word by word*, and then she would correct my pronunciation. Albeit fastidious, this is the right way to learn a language. Pleasant immersion. Her mother also made tasty Mexican food from scratch.

As I had joined the wrestling team during my freshman year at Riverside, I thought training in judo could be useful and would keep me in good shape. So, I enrolled in a judo school in Maracaibo, taught by Sensei Yves Carouget. Sensei Carouget was the first teacher to bring judo and aikido to Venezuela, and he held advanced-level black belts in judo, aikido, jujitsu and also karate. I was fortunate to train under him for three summers. In the many years since, Sensei Carouget has become something of a legend in martial arts circles. I found him to be an excellent and tough instructor and a very nice man.

An Excursion to Colombia

During the summer of 1965, I went with Augusto to Colombia for a few weeks. To save money, we travelled by car, bus and airplane. Augusto's father, Napo, drove us three hours from Maracaibo to Maicao, a Colombian frontier town near the Venezuelan border. We did a little shopping for clothes that could be obtained there for half the price of similar items in Venezuela.

Then on to Villanueva by bus, where Augusto had several close relatives. We spent a delightful day at his Uncle Miguel's farm, called "La Victoria," where we rode horses and enjoyed delicious barbeque. Villanueva reminded me of a scene from the American Old West, where cowboys rode horses into town and tied them up in front of the general store. But the highlight for me was meeting Augusto's extended family. A salt of the earth kind of people. Every time he greeted a relative, a mutual shower of affection commenced.

As our goal was to fly to Bogotá and as there was not an airport in Villanueva, on we went by bus to Valledupar, a brief 38-mile trek. At the Valledupar airport, we were advised that Colombian commercial pilots were on strike, and no flights were available. And so, we boarded another bus and continued on our merry way for an additional 180 miles to Barranquilla.

Though we were very tired from riding crowded busses for over 200 miles, on arrival in Barranquilla, we went to the airport, where Augusto's cousin, Nancy Ferreira, worked as a ticket agent. "Sorry, my loves," she said to us. "The commercial pilots are still on national strike."

Tired and out of options, we took a cab to the downtown Barranquilla area. We found a hotel that set us back $4 for the night. If you look up the word "ugly" in the dictionary, you should find a picture of our rundown hotel room. Dingy. Two small beds. Lumpy mattresses. No air conditioning.

We found a store and purchased a big bottle of 60-proof Cristal aguardiente, the national drink of Colombia, similar to but hotter than French anisette. Armed with the medication, we entered a movie theater that boldly advertised, "Aire Acondicionado." And there we sat, chugging aguardiente, loving the AC and watching John Wayne speak Spanish.

At the conclusion of the double feature, we had to leave the theater. It was evening by then, and with the sun down, the temperature had dropped a bit. Our hotel room was still hot, so we would talk for a while, take a shower to cool down, take a swig of aguardiente and repeat. After three or four cycles of this numbing and cooling-down process, we thought we might try to sleep.

I fell asleep sometime after 2 AM, dreaming, I am sure, of skiing on the frozen slope of a white mountain in Alaska. After an hour or two, I was awakened. Something was on my leg. No idea what. It was big. Crawling up my thigh. It had lots of legs. I could not take the terror any longer. Jumping out of bed, I screamed and flung the creature from my body. Turning on the room light, there it was in the middle of the floor... a giant cockroach. A horrible monster as big as a baseball with six legs. And now, the devil was trying to get away. About two seconds later, the monster went to meet his maker.

We did not sleep much that night. In the following morning, promptly at dawn, we showered and ate our breakfast. We checked out of the Hotel Cucaracha, and hailed a taxi to take us to the airport. Fortunately, Augusto's cousin was on duty. "Nancy," we asked, "are there commercial flights today?"

"I am so sorry," Nancy replied, "the strike continues."
"But Nancy, we have to go to Bogotá today! Please, is there anything?"
"I am sorry," she repeated. "the only flight to Bogotá today is a cargo plane."
"Well, can you put us on that?"
"It would be very uncomfortable," she replied. "There are no seats."
"We don't care," Augusto said. "We will take anything."
"Okay, then," she declared. "Please step on the scale."

Which we did. Augusto and I each stood on the scale, and we paid the fare based on our physical weight. The cost was $40 for both of us. We said our thank you's and goodbye's to lovely Nancy and boarded the freight plane, with our paid cargo manifest in hand. A VW station wagon was on the craft, and its doors were unlocked. So, we entered the car, put the seats back and passed the aguardiente. Flying over the cold Andes, the drink kept us warm, and the bouncy propeller plane arrived at the Bogotá airport two hours later.

We had a terrific time, staying with Augusto's grandparents in a grand old house in a nice Bogotá neighborhood. Nestled in the Andes at an altitude of 8,600 feet, the city typically remains a pleasant 65 degrees in July. We took in a bull fight, and I learned the way to hold and angle a bota to drink wine. We paid a visit to the extraordinary Gold Museum, which contains the largest collection of prehispanic gold in the world. We visited an architectural miracle, the Salt Cathedral, nationally proclaimed as "The First Wonder of Colombia." I was honored to sit in a chair owned by the Great Liberator, Simón Bolívar.

We went to a two-story, packed pub, where everybody sang along with the artist on stage. After one hour of pleading, the artist/MC finally accepted a request for my favorite Latin song; I can still hear those 300 voices raising "Cielito Lindo" to the heavens. Finally, as a justified thank you to Augusto's grandparents, we arranged a serenade for them by Colombian folk singers. Unfortunately, at 2 AM.

And then it was time for us to return to Maracaibo and time for me to return to Riverside. My senior year at the military academy was my most enjoyable period there, but I was ecstatic to graduate on May 31, 1966. After four years of marching and saluting, I was on my way home to Venezuela.

Back in Maracaibo, I resumed the study of judo under the tutelage of Sensei Carouget. And then, I was invited to join a rock band. From late 1966 until 1968, I was honored to be the lead singer of a popular group, "Los Hippies."

Our Maracaibo band also featured Carlos Moreno (lead guitar and vocals), Leopoldo Bohorque (bass) and Edgardo Carroz (drums). We performed music by the Beatles, Rolling Stones and many others. Carlos ("Carlitos") was a gifted guitarist. On hearing a new song for the first time, he would play it flawlessly on the first attempt. A few of the songs in our repertoire included: "As Tears Go By" (Stones), "Good Lovin'" (Rascals), "It Won't Be Long" (Beatles), "House of the Rising Sun" (Animals), "Like A Rolling Stone" (Dylan) and "Love Potion #9" (Searchers).

Our manager, Léon, booked gigs for us at most of the popular venues in town, including Club Bella Vista, Club Milagro, Club Náutico and Club Comercio. We made a little money and had an absolute blast playing for the teen crowd. The music of the latter sixties was a fusion of introversion and extroversion, and artists were communicating their most intimate thoughts and feelings, poetically, through melodic music. The Venezuelan youth of the era knew something was going on, and they wanted to be part of it.

I recall one special night with Los Hippies. Léon, had booked two gigs for the band that evening, about four miles apart. We played six songs at Club Bella Vista, and then ran to the station wagon with guitars and drumsticks in hand. Léon rushed us to the second show, a young lady's Quinceañera celebration, where another set of Fender amps awaited.

After we spilled out of the car like The Monkees, Carlitos plugged in and attacked the opening riff to the rocker, "Roll Over Beethoven." As we belted out, *Gonna write a little letter / Gonna mail it to my local DJ*, those joyful Maracuchos danced like their lives depended on it. That evening and the sixties were a blur for Los Hippies, partly due to Léon's driving.

After the parties ended, late at night, Augusto and I would drive to the northern outskirts of Maracaibo to Puerto Caballo, a modest restaurant by the lake. They served fresh fish caught that day. We would order the wood-grilled, whole catfish with yucca for 2 Bs. (47 US cents.) I do cherish that memory. A cool breeze blowing. A silver moon reflecting on the crystal-clear water. A delicious meal with good friends, Jorge Hernández and Germán Parra.

The US Army lassoed me in January of 1968, and I was ordered to report to the draft board in America. I served my time in the military, and afterwards, life would take me in several directions. Since then, over these past 50 years, I have returned to Maracaibo a few times. Though I am a native Californian, I did not leave my heart in San Francisco. When I close my tired, old eyes, my heart returns to the Venezuela that was.

Oh my, the Venezuela that was. A stable government. A stable economy. A country making improvements in infrastructure. A highly educated people. Super safe streets. Inexpensive public transportation. Inexpensive and delicious food. A substantial and happy middle class with a solid future.

The Venezuela That Is
Since my family left Venezuela, what has changed?

Everything. In an effort to control its destiny by controlling its most valuable resource, the country's oil industry was nationalized in 1976. While the idea of a state-owned oil industry, independent of foreign influence, started as a means of dictating the country's destiny, it ended up as the beginning of its downfall. Nationalization as a *concept* is compelling, but losing technical assistance from America, Germany and the Netherlands has proved catastrophic.

Tragically, life in Venezuela has deteriorated to the brink of near collapse, primarily due to two kamikaze pilots: Hugo Chávez and Nicolás Maduro. Serving as President of Venezuela from 1999-2013, Chávez aligned himself with the Marxist-Leninist governments of Fidel and then Raúl Castro in Cuba. Being a prominent adversary of the United States, Chávez described his quixotic policies as anti-imperialist.

Due to the death of Chávez in 2013, Vice President Nicolás Maduro assumed the Presidency, and he remains in that position today. During Maduro's reign, according to the National Union of Press Workers of Venezuela, 115 media outlets have been shut down. And since 2019, Venezuela has been exposed to frequent "information blackouts," periods without access to internet or news services during important political events. What is Maduro hiding?

Everything. Employment has plummeted. Salaries are a fraction of what they were, and according to the BBC, 75% of Venezuelans live in extreme poverty.

Prices have rocketed. For 2019, the World Bank estimated inflation at 10 million percent! The ATMs went empty. The gas stations are empty. Research by Caritas shows 70% of the children show signs of malnutrition. And according to *New Yorker* magazine, Venezuela has the world's highest violent crime rate. Even stairwells in a hospital are not safe from robbers, who prey on staff and patients.

As documented by the United Nations, under Maduro's rule, more than 9,000 people have been subject to extrajudicial killings, and almost 6 million Venezuelans have been forced to flee the country. Many of them walked out to neighboring countries... to Colombia, Panama and Brazil. Included in the catastrophically long list of political refugees is Augusto's oldest daughter, Alexandra, who escaped to the United States with her family in 2015.

Maduro's crimes against everybody and everything continue. In 2020, the US Department of Justice indicted him on charges of drug trafficking and narco-terrorism, and the US Department of State has offered a $15 million reward for information that helps bring the criminal to justice. Who supports Maduro? Russia, China, Iran, Syria and Cuba.

What about beautiful Lake Maracaibo? Local biologist Alejandro Álvarez said, "It's like living next to a toilet. Nothing good can come of that." Smelling like an oil refinery, the vast expanse of Lake Maracaibo has become grossly polluted by its own reserves of crude, as Venezuela's economic collapse has left wells and pipelines in ruin.

How could this happen? A telling report from Transparency International: Venezuela ranks 176th out of 180 countries on their 2021 Corruption Index. Maduro and his cronies, fugitives from justice, safe in the presidential palace, under the protection of elite Cuban security forces, continue to enjoy Russian caviar and Cuban cigars... while the people die.

Earlier in this article, Chávez and Maduro were referred to as kamikaze pilots. That is not exactly correct. They kill everything *except themselves*.

My heart goes out to my Venezuelan brothers and sisters.

My final words are for Mr. Maduro and his willing followers:
Crimes against humanity.
Crimes against nature.
Crimes against God.

THE RIVERSIDE CADET:
LIFE IN A MILITARY ACADEMY

During the first year we lived in Maracaibo, I had enjoyed myself too much. So, when the teacher handed me the sealed envelope addressed to Mr. and Mrs. Ziemer, I knew there would be repercussions.

Dad and Mom were disappointed in the massive amount of red ink on my 8th grade report card. As the 1962-63 school year was drawing near, they agreed that I should transfer to a private school. Dad's good friend and colleague, Blackie Armel, who lived across the street from us, had a well-mannered son, Steve, who was a four-year senior at Riverside Military Academy in Georgia. The decision was made to enroll me in the all-boys institution.

All I realized at 13 years of age was that I was leaving my Venezuela home, and soon, I would be in military uniform. I hated to leave my sister Paulette, who depended on me for many things. But I liked Steve. He told me that he would keep an eye on me, and I would be fine. I said goodbye to my friends, hugged my family and marched to the airplane that would take me to America.

Much to my dismay, the Pam American turbo-prop departed on schedule. Soon, we were flying over the Caribbean Sea and enjoying turquoise textures, on our way to Miami, the southern gateway to the USA. About 30 minutes outside of Miami, the pilot announced we had a "major problem" and would have to make an emergency landing in Havana, 90 miles from the US shore.

A little perspective. The date is September 7, 1962. Following the disastrous Bay of Pigs invasion, tensions between the United States, Russia and Cuba remain at an all-time high. The players are John Kennedy, Nikita Khrushchev and Fidel Castro. The Cuban Missile Crisis, arguably the scariest event in human history, will command center stage in just 37 days. That showdown will bring the world's two superpowers to the brink of nuclear war.

Back to our airplane in trouble. The pilot tells us the Havana tower is not giving us permission to land, but our pilot has no choice. We touch down on the Cuban runway and are immediately surrounded by armored vehicles, two on each side of the craft. The airliner comes to a stop. The door opens. Two bearded guerillas in green fatigues and military caps enter the plane. With machine guns.

A few more Castro clones establish a perimeter of surveillance on the tarmac. There we stay for four hours while Cuban mechanics work on the airplane. The cabin door remains open, and the inside temperature reaches at least 110 degrees. We are ordered to remain in our seats. The two bearded guerillas appear to be just as nervous as the passengers.

After an hour or two, stewardesses are given permission to serve water to the hot passengers. Shortly thereafter, hands go up, and one by one, people are allowed to visit the restroom. When my turn comes, I do the stupidest thing... I sneak my Kodak camera into the restroom and snap three or four pictures of the Havana airport.

Six weeks later, a US Air Force "U-2" reconnaissance aircraft - a spy plane - piloted by Major Rudy Anderson, would be shot down over Cuba for presumably taking pictures of secret launch sites of nuclear weapons. This event would be the definitive straw to almost break the camel's back in triggering a nuclear war between the US and Russia. What if one of the guards had caught me "shooting" his airport?

But I remember thinking how clever I was. Maybe the volcanic heat had something to do with my lack of judgement. Whatever. It was very stupid. In due course, the guerillas exited the airplane, and we departed for Miami. Once we had "wheels up," everybody on board cheered.

Reaching Miami four hours late caused me to miss my connection to Atlanta, but another Delta flight was available a short time later. On arrival at the single terminal in Atlanta, I met two cadets who were on their way to Riverside. We agreed to share a cab to the academy.

The towering red brick buildings were intimidating and the first thing I noticed, once we reached the sprawling campus. Resting in the foothills of the Blue Ridge Mountains, the school is located 50 miles from Atlanta in Gainesville. With a stunning backdrop of majestic Lake Lanier and soaring pine trees, Riverside's 206-acre site is equally impressive and imposing. And adequately isolated to accomplish goals of the institution.

Since the school began in 1908 with an enrollment of two cadets, the goal has remained the same: to instill discipline, build character and build leaders. The goal is reflected in the academy's motto, "mens sana in corpore sano," Latin for "a sound mind in a sound body." Funky words to a 13-year-old kid.

But on this gray day, September 7, 1962, a century after the Civil War began, I felt like a little pig going to slaughter, and at five feet short and 102 pounds wet, I did my best to stand a bit taller. Two sergeants or generals (I did not know the difference) were seated at the check-in table. "Hello," said I in my deepest voice. "My name is Joe Ziemer."

"Welcome, Cadet Ziemer. We have your packet of information right here. You have been assigned to 'E' Company, and your room in East Barracks is over there. Cadet Smith will show you to your room." Surely, they could hear my heart pounding? Did I have any color in my face? As Cadet Smith led me to my quarters, I was certain he was smiling at how green I looked.

The "E" Company barracks were very old with a red brick facia and gray wood hallways and stairways. I could sense the timeworn character emanating from the structure. There were two floors containing about 50 cadet rooms. My room on the main level had wood floors, a wood closet, a wood desk, one set of bunkbeds and a cast-iron radiator that delivered steam heat.

When I opened the door, a boy was sitting at a desk, spitting on his shoes. This would be my roommate: Oscar Rodriguez, a 6 ft. tall guy, a sophomore. Oscar was from Miami, of Cuban descent, and he was beginning his second year at Riverside. He had achieved the rank of corporal. Oscar was intrigued by my experience in Havana, and he wanted to know all about life in Maracaibo. This was great. I had many questions, and Oscar seemed nice.

My roommate was not a luck-of-the-draw situation. The academy attempts to pair new kids with "old boys" who know the ropes and can pass on their survival skills. As a new kid on the block, it was an instant morale boost to know my roommate had survived the first year.

Over the next day, the academy made me one of their own. My Elvis-like ducktail quickly fell to the barbershop floor. In its place, a clean crew cut. We waited in endless lines for chow, uniforms, physical checkups and class schedules. The first full day was so jampacked, we did not have time to change our minds. But looking at new cadets made me feel better, knowing we were in the same boat. I could see that we were not headed to slaughter, but we were definitely being herded and branded. Exhausted but thankful that the day was finished, I remember lying in the darkness, listening to the bugler play the loneliest tune in the world, "Taps."

Morning came too soon, as the bugler blew "Reveille" on his shrill trumpet. Oscar said inspection would be in 20 minutes. He had already helped me to shine my shoes and brass, organize my foot locker and closet; and he also showed me how to make a bed with regulation hospital corners. We stood at attention at the head of our bunks, as the two inspectors entered our room. Lieutenant Sullivan, our resident faculty advisor and our cadet company commander told us that our room looked good. And then Oscar said we had to run. We hurried to the quad, where the cadet battalion was forming.

Oscar showed me where my company, platoon and squad were assembling, and I joined the military formation with fellow cadets. All 600 cadets were in uniform. Gray trousers with black stripes. Gray long-sleeve shirts with brass insignia on the collar. Black ties tucked into the shirt at the third button down from the collar. Black belts with shiny brass buckles. Black lace-up shoes. Army garrison caps. And of course, name tags. Mine read "ZIEMER."

This formation occurred twice a day, Monday through Friday. At 7:30 AM and 6:00 PM, cadets came together in battalion formation in front of Lanier Hall. Roll was taken to confirm all boys were present. Each cadet was inspected. The uniform had to be clean and pressed; shoes had to be shined; brass had to be polished. Following the inspection, platoons would march on the quad until their turn came to enter the mess hall.

A faculty member or cadet officer headed up each table in the mess hall, where the food was plentiful and nutritious. Gainesville is known as "Chicken Capitol of the World," and to promote their poultry, in 1961, the City Council voted to make it illegal to eat fried chicken with a fork! I can still picture metal trays filled with chicken, grits and SOS (shit-on-a-shingle). Three square meals per day were served with milk, juice, coffee and sometimes dessert.

One point struck me the first time we were assembled together on the quad: All cadets, faculty and regular Army military staff were White. Considering that Riverside is located in the Deep South... when I started there in 1962... Black boys were not admitted. In the local host city, Gainesville, I recall seeing separate drinking fountains and seating areas for Blacks and Whites. Though it was a sign of the times in the Deep South, this was foreign to me. Such divisions were predominantly nonexistent in California and Venezuela. But to be completely clear, though Riverside's mess-hall workers were Black, in my time at the academy, I did not witness any act of derogatory behavior towards a Black employee.

There was so much to take in at Riverside, so much to learn and so much to get used to. The marching. The saluting. The inspections. The rules and regulations. The do this and do not do that. The terribly busy schedule.

Though I did not realize it at the time, I would come to see that a structured routine is not just strenuous, but it can bring comfort. Strenuous to new cadets because at first it is chaotic. Comforting to new cadets because they are too busy running to think about anything else. In time, the routine becomes a natural rhythm, and in this structure, a boy can thrive.

The weekday schedule played a crucial role in the regimentation of the cadet, and activities were marked by a continual ringing of bells throughout the day:

AM	6:45	Reveille (wake up)
	7:05	Room inspection
	7:30	Mess formation (for breakfast)
	8:00	Chapel formation
	8:30	Classes begin
PM	12:00	Lunch
	1:00	Classes resume
	2:30	Military drill (marching with M-1 rifles)
	4:00	Athletics
	5:30	Call to quarters (shower, clean room, etc.)
	6:00	Mess formation (for dinner)
	7:00	Retreat (evening inspection)
	7:30	Study hall
	9:45	Tattoo (prepare for bed)
	10:00	Taps (lights out)

This was the normal schedule for weekday activities. Cadets in good standing were allowed to go into town (Gainesville) on Wednesday afternoons for four hours and on Saturdays for seven hours. On Sundays, there was a formal room inspection by the Commandant and a cadet military parade in full dress.

The bulk of the week day, about seven hours, was spent in class and in study. Every cadet was required to take four major subjects and also a military class. The academy promoted itself as a college preparatory school, and rightly so. The student-to-teacher ratio was a very low 12:1, and following graduation, 95% of students would go on to attend a four-year college.

Though Riverside Military Academy (RMA) has been a fully certified **military** academy since 1923, the importance of academics to the institution cannot be understated. In the handbook titled *Cadet Regulations* (the cadet bible), it states, Riverside's "chief aim is the furtherance of academic interests... and major emphasis is placed on satisfactory advancement of each cadet."

This "advancement" was accomplished through a five-point incentive system:
(1) Grades were mailed home **every week** and posted publicly.
(2) Good grades were one of the factors that led to military promotion.
(3) Cadets were given an allowance for the average of their weekly grades:

0-69	$1.00
70-79	$2.00
80-89	$3.00
90-94	$4.00
95-100	$5.00

(4) Good grades were the quickest way to acquire merits, or points for good behavior, which could be spent on special privileges, such as town privileges.

(5) If a student failed a class during the week with a grade below 70, he was required to attend study hall. Despised by cadets, "The Pit" was a large room with 200-300 cadets with instructors patrolling the aisles.

Really, for the very first time in my very short life, I was being forced to study. It was a terribly difficult and painful undertaking in the beginning. My student load during the first year was standard curriculum for a high-school freshman: History I, Algebra I, English 1, General Science, and Military I. Though the subject matter was not difficult, the newness and strangeness of academy life made everything difficult.

And then there was the military side. We learned how to salute, polish brass, tie a necktie and shave (peach fuzz at the time). We continually marched with M-1 rifles and learned how to strip them and clean them and put them back together. We became experts at shining shoes. To put a "mirror shine" on shoes, five elements are required: Kiwi black shoe polish, a flannel cloth, spit and water. And hours of sweat. During my four years at RMA, I spent 18 days shining shoes. All of this was mandatory. Our rooms and our personal appearance were inspected by higher ranking cadets twice a day or more. We constantly cleaned everything. The floor. The desk. The sink. The toilet. The walls. The showers. The stairs. The hallways. The grounds.

Like all new kids at RMA, I was at the bottom of the totem pole. It seemed as if any cadet could command me to scrub the toilet or police up cigarette butts. I understood pretty quickly that the bottom was a despicable place to be. Cadets with rank seemed confident and happier. Rank started at lowly private ("pee-on"), who was basically in charge of nothing, and ascended to colonel, who was over the battalion of 600 cadets. Rank was achieved through good soldiering, good grades, good deportment and accrued time at RMA.

CADET RANK	APPROX. #	IN CHARGE OF
Private	350	Himself
Private First Class	50	Team - 5 cadets
Corporal	25	Ditto
Sergeant	25	Ditto or a squad (10 cadets)
Sergeant First Class	65	Squad
Master Sergeant	20	Assists platoon leader
First Sergeant	8	Assists company commander
Second Lieutenant	20	Platoon - 3 squads
First Lieutenant	8	Assists company commander
Captain	8	Company - 3 platoons
Major	1	Assists battalion commander
Lieutenant Colonel	1	Battalion - 7 companies

Riverside's Junior Reserve Officer Training Corps (JROTC) program is one of the most prestigious in America. For 80 years, it has been designated as an Honor Unit with Distinction. The hierarchical structure consisted of seven companies, A-F, plus the band. I was assigned to "E" Company, 3rd Platoon, 3rd Squad. In every private's chain of command, several cadets held rank over him and could command him to "get in step." Cadet Ziemer, like 349 other privates, had zero status, plus he had to do exactly what he was told.

How did the academy control a boy's behavior? Completely explained in the *Cadet Regulations*, the demerit system was an effective hammer to keep boys in line. Whenever a cadet deviated from the rules of the academy, he could be "burned with D's" (given demerits). A cadet could be burned for such offenses as dirty fingernails (one demerit), trash in can (two demerits), laughing in ranks (five demerits), blowing horn in barracks (10), shooting paper wads (15), civilian clothes in locker (20), changing color of hair (25), smoking without (parental) permission (50), use of a private automobile (75) and "breaking barracks" - sneaking out of the barracks after lights out - (100). The *Cadet Regulations* lists 359 offenses for which a cadet could be burned.

If any cadet received over 35 demerits in a week, the mandatory punishment, enforced by the Commandant's Office, was to walk the Wednesday/Saturday "Bull Ring." Each demerit over 35 corresponded to 20 minutes. So, if a cadet received 50 demerits, he would walk in nonstop circles for five straight hours. Fear of the Bull Ring was effective motivation for a cadet to stay out of trouble, and from the academy's viewpoint, it was a powerful agent of social control.

Any cadet with rank, who received 50 demerits in a week, could be reduced to the grade of private and transferred from his present company to another company in different barracks. Being stripped publicly of achieved rank was not only deflating and embarrassing, but it also meant lower ranking cadets then became one's superiors.

Any cadet could give demerits to a lower ranking individual. A 14-year-old private first class could command a 19-year-old private to sweep the hall or clean his fingernails. If the order was not followed, the offender could be burned. Indeed, for the military chain-of-command system to work effectively, orders from higher ranking individuals must be followed, regardless of age. However, cadets who were too quick and too frequent with the demerit pad would acquire the precarious title, "chicken-shit." The boys had their own way of dealing with these cadets. Fear of getting hammered loomed large.

As a pee-on with no status, I felt the weight of all this. The crushing schedule. Must get good grades. Scrub the floor. Shine the shoes. Time to wake up. Time to go to sleep. Eat now. Listen up. Hurry up. Attention! At Ease. Hup-two-three-four! Get in step, Private! I will burn your ass! Hup-two-three-four!

Most certainly, these bizarre people were out of their minds. They were out there on their own aberrated wavelength, and Cadet Ziemer was in an inextricable situation. Even though I loathed academy life, with Oscar's help, I had managed to stay out of trouble. After about three weeks at Riverside, the gravity of my predicament hit me. I remember lying in the darkness, crying. I had never felt so defenseless, and I wanted to go home.

Out of the blue, the sergeant-of-the-guard entered my room and announced, "Ziemer, you have an emergency phone call." I jumped out of bed, dressed quickly and ran to the guardhouse. Mom was on the phone; she was in Miami with Paulette. Mom said she and Dad had separated and she was on her way to California to be with her father, Dewey. She said she would file for divorce, and it was all for the best. Mom said she loved me, and that was it.

My memory is blank on what transpired during the remainder of the evening. In the morning, during my first class, I was ordered to report to the Registrar's Office, to Colonel James Mooney, the second highest ranking staff member. "Joe," he said, "your mother telephoned me this morning and explained the situation. I am so sorry, son."

His words pierced me and the dam exploded. I broke down and told him everything. That I hated this crazy place. That I did not belong at Riverside. That I wanted to go home.

"Joe," he replied, looking into my eyes, "I know life at Riverside can be hard. But we want you to stay here, and we want this to become your second home. I will do everything in my power to help you."

"If you wish," he said, "I will speak with the student counselor, Lt. Sullivan. His residence is in your company barracks, a few doors down from your room. Lt. Sullivan will be happy to work with you, Joe, and my door is always open. We want you to succeed, son."

Colonel Mooney's sincere words enveloped me like the soothing water of Lake Maracaibo. At a time when my world had collapsed, he stood tall in his concern for my wellbeing. It truly seemed that Mr. Naiveté had an ally or two. As I returned to class, I stepped quicker, and the grounds were more in focus.

Later that evening, during the 7 PM room inspection, I got burned for my shoes under the bed not being shined on the back heel. Funny thing was, the infraction did not dishearten me.

During "Chapel" the following morning, the Owner of Riverside (since 1913), General Sandy Beaver, addressed the corps. He was a tall, imposing man, and he often spoke at assemblies. Towering above the podium, General Beaver said, "We want you to like us and believe that you will; but we are more concerned as to what your mature opinion of us will be in 10 years."

Something clicked in my head, and one could say that I had an epiphany. There was not a personal vendetta against me... Life was not out to get me. The academy with its strict regimen was designed to be difficult for all cadets, and Riverside was too mighty for any cadet to fight. The only way that I could prevail was to join the party. I was tired of being down, and I wanted to win. This pee-on decided he was going to get some respect.

I needed to get the school's schedule under control. It was destroying me, and I had to find some way to get ahead of the curve. So, I did something unimaginable to most 13-year-old kids. I woke up at 5 AM.

New boys were exhausted at the end of a typical day, and waking up at the programmed time (6:45) was difficult. So, when the alarm sounded at 5:00 in the morning, it took all of my strength to roll out of bed. Repetition made the process easier, and after three or four early mornings, I woke up before the clock screamed. But the first week was tough.

My early mornings would begin with a cup of coffee, instantly made in my room with an illegal heat 'n' coil (25 demerits if caught). I would place blankets around my bottom bunk bed, so the bright pen light would not awaken Oscar. I would study until 6 AM, then shine my shoes, clean my brass and shower. When reveille sounded at 6:45, I was ready to face the world.

After a few weeks of rising before the birds, I was feeling better about my course work. When Saturday morning arrived, I ran to the bulletin board to see my posted grades. With an average of 95%, I had made the honor roll. Later that day, when allowances were paid, I received the maximum amount, five dollars. In Chapel assembly two days later, Col. Mooney announced the names of cadets who had made the weekly honor roll, and he asked them to stand on the stage and face the cadet corps.

For the first time in my universe, studying was beneficial, as it led to more money, praise and freedom. Having a few greenbacks in my pocket allowed me to enjoy my favorite campus hangout, The Grill. A tasty cheeseburger, french fries and milkshake could be had for $1.25. What's more, a Seeburg jukebox stood in the corner, where one quarter would buy three loud songs. In 1962, "Sherry" by the 4 Seasons and "Do You Love Me" by The Contours were popular selections. A few cadets would even dance. The Grill provided a much-needed escape. It was an oasis, and good grades got me there.

Before coming to Riverside, I had never really studied nor had I read a major novel. I read The Grapes of Wrath in my first semester and was fascinated to discover the plight of my Okie relatives. Reading and studying became more than a paycheck. The books became *interesting*.

By creating more time, my plan was working. Success came by studying without distraction, and shining shoes, cleaning the room and staying in step.

Over the next eight weeks, before the cadet corps would break for Christmas, I would make the honor roll almost every week.

I quickly grew to depend on Riverside for my very existence. The academy provided the key necessities: food, shelter, discipline and social structure. Its time-proven routine and well-oiled mechanisms - to keep the boy focused on the here and now - were incredibly effective. Getting with *that* program taught me to focus on the world in front of me, and the rewards were swift. As a result, the mess hall became Mom's kitchen, and my significance for the word "home" would change.

Unwinding

Like The Grill, sports gave cadets a break from the rigors of academy life. Participation in athletics was required from 4:00 - 5:30, four days per week. Cadets could try out for a team, such as basketball or opt for intramural sports. In the first semester, I wrestled and played freshman football.

Though I was short, I had speed, so the football coach made me an offensive end. The main function of the position is as an eligible receiver downfield, meaning the offensive end runs out for passes and hopefully catches them. During the first game of the season, the coach put me in as a *defensive* end, meaning the other team had the ball, and my primary job was to stop an end run or break up an end pass.

As teams lined up in formation, I noticed the end I was guarding was huge. The guy had to be over 6 feet tall and weigh 200 pounds. At twice my weight, he had long arms like a gorilla and beady red eyes. He spit on the ground and asked, "Are you scared, kid?"

Yes, I was. But I could not let him know. I looked at him and said, "Let's go!"

First play, the quarterback throws the ball to the giant. I go for the tackle and bounce off his legs. He bolts by me and starts galloping downfield. I catch up and jump on his back. I ride him like a jockey. Five yards, ten yards... I wrestle him to the ground, and he lands on top of me. The next thing I hear, "Joe, how many fingers am I holding up?" When I am able to walk back to the bench, my teammates slap me on the back. I had taken the ogre down.

To pick on boys my own size, I joined the Riverside wrestling team. At the time, my weight was 102 pounds, which put me in the lightest weight class. Though my wrestling skills were average at best, the meets were exciting. And I felt great being in the best physical shape of my life.

In addition to sports, there were several opportunities for a cadet to unwind. If a boy were in good academic standing, the second hour of study hall on weekdays could be used to visit another cadet. Or sleep. On Wednesday afternoons, chapel, athletics and drill were not scheduled, so cadets could use that time freely. Saturdays were free as well, unless the cadet had a date with Study Hall or the Bull Ring.

On Wednesdays and Saturdays, the boys were permitted to travel into town. Once a cadet passed a personal inspection, he would board the Riverside bus for a short five-minute ride into Gainesville. And what did we do there? We checked out the girls. Now and then, we would run into a young lady from Brenau, a private girls' academy located about three miles from Riverside. If one were lucky, the young Miss might want to see a movie.

Cadets wandering the streets of Gainesville had to maintain a steady lookout for town boys, which we referred to as "mice." (We were Riverside "Rats.") Town boys prowled the streets in cars, like a pack of wolves, searching for an isolated cadet. When one was spotted, mice would spill out of the car, strike the cadet and steal his military hat. This happened to a friend, Cadet Wade Inman. The feud with town boys gave cadets a strong sense of solidarity. (Interesting point of human nature the way a common enemy, real or perceived, tends to unite discordant people.)

A popular hangout that united cadets was Woolworth's, a five-and-dime store on Washington Street on the town square. Yummy banana splits could be had for one to 31 cents... Just pick a balloon. If a cadet had made the weekly honor roll, he could also afford a cheeseburger and fries.

Step outside the store, and a cadet might meet up with a corner preacher. Gainesville had one who wore a bright white suit with a black western bowtie. Add a white goatee, and the guy could have passed for Colonel Sanders. Heaven help the child who fell under his gaze, for the man would shout, "Listen to me, sinner! You will burn in the fires of hell!"

While the fire-and-brimstone preacher was on his own lordly wavelength, he was an amusing spectacle to teenage cadets. With corner preachers, enemy mice, movie theaters, pretty girls and banana splits... town days gave cadets a much-needed break from the rigors of academy life.

Social Status and Peer-Group Pressure

Receiving a perfumed letter from a girl was another pick-me-up that helped soothe the mental stress of academy life. It did not matter what the letter said. Giving cadets a whiff of a sweet-smelling letter would always bring a smile, and it was a nice status boost, regardless of rank. Receiving a "care package" from home was also a big deal. It gave a cadet instant power in deciding who would be offered a valuable homemade brownie. My family mailed me several care packages, roughly one per month, filled with delectable goodies. And loads of See's candy.

We should keep in mind that Riverside was an all-boys school, and outside the mechanisms of rank and control, the boys had their own set of rules to determine social status. High on the list... a positive correlation existed between strength/toughness and a cadet's social position. The best athletes, for instance, were highly respected. Likewise, a quick way to boost standing was for a Rat to fight a mouse *in self-defense* and win. Finally, most any boy who was considered to be a "ladies' man" was envied by a majority of cadets. "Machismo" is the word for these examples.

The reverse was true, as well. While in today's liberal era it is not politically correct to say, but as we are discussing a situation that existed 60 years ago, the assumed homosexual faced an uphill climb in attempting to gain respect; any cadet caught in homosexual activity would be expelled immediately. Similarly, an effeminate boy had a hard time climbing the social ladder.

Gung-ho and chicken-s--- cadets were largely despised. But the lowest position in the social pecking order was reserved for extremely gross cadet. Companies competed with each other in drills and inspections, and the weekly winner was awarded the privilege of eating first in the mess hall and sleeping late on Sunday. One gross cadet could ruin a company's chance to win, and *that* would impact 90 cadets. Therefore, the gross cadet was uniformly blasted, and in social status, he was the lowest of the low. Responsibility would fall on the squad leader and roommates to help the gross cadet clean up his act.

If a boy could beat the system without causing harm to another cadet, the perceived cleverness could give him a bump up in status. Examples of respected acts of deviance follow, but smoking cigarettes is the best example. 16-year-old boys were allowed to smoke if they had parental permission. Illegal smoking, then, was done by younger cadets - cautiously - since it was a 50-demerit offense, and the regulation was strictly enforced. But boys will be boys, and peer-group pressure in a military school is formidable.

And what about alcohol? Gainesville is located in Hall County, a "dry" county at the time, meaning booze was not sold publicly in stores. I have read that moonshine was available in "them thar hills" and from some local farmers. But we had no dealings with farmers. So, if a cadet wanted a taste, what would he do? A wild and crazy kid just might strain 26-proof Aqua Velva through bread and drink it. The blue lips were a dead giveaway.

In all seriousness, I can count on one hand the number of times I witnessed alcohol *on campus*. If a cadet were caught, the penalty was expulsion. So, drinking was done off campus, away from the prying eyes of the academy. In four years, I did not hear of an instance of drug use. But this was a conservative era and a few years before the Summer of Love.

In certain peer groups, breaking barracks was a "respected" act of deviance, providing the boy did not get caught. The cadet would sneak out of his room after taps to go on a pizza run, a Dairy Queen run or to visit a coed at the Brenau school for girls. When the runner returned with pizza or ice cream, his customers applauded, and the runner's social status would go up a notch. But If he were caught, the penalty was severe, 100 demerits or expulsion.

After living with 600 boys for four years, I recognize that social position did not always correspond to military rank. But it was just as real. Social position was earned positively (good athlete, for example) or negatively (pizza runner). The Riverside life was defined by strict routines and demands of the academy, but social pressure, good or bad, was a powerful motivator.

Stated another way, social pressure began where rank ended. A concerned cadet could plead with his buddy not to break barracks. Boys would also find a way to "take care" of the gross or chicken-s--- cadet, the one who refused to straighten up and fly right. Persuasive kids, representing what was best for the cadet corps, could often correct a situation that the school could not.

A Warmer Atmosphere

As my first quarter at RMA was ending in December of 1962, I was proud of what I had accomplished. Three months earlier, a scared kid with no standing had entered the academy. Oscar and Col. Mooney had helped me through an especially tough time. And even though I did not sleep much, I learned how to study, and my progress was promptly reflected in A-level report cards. Meanwhile, the temperature in Gainesville was dropping into the low 40's, and as we broke out the winter coats ("reefers"), I was looking forward to spending a warm Christmas with Mom and sister Paulette in California.

Spending time with my family was exactly what the doctor ordered. I was overjoyed to see that Mom had bounced back from her difficulties, and she was in great spirits. She had found a good job that she enjoyed, and Paulette was doing well in the first grade. I was "pumped" and ready to carry on.

I actually looked forward to returning to the academy for the second season. But I did not travel back to Gainesville. I caught a flight to Miami and took a taxi to Hollywood-By-The-Sea, Florida. The coastal city served as the host-location of Riverside's winter campus for January, February and half of March. During these months, Hollywood was 25 degrees warmer than Gainesville, which permitted drills and sports to be conducted outside.

Not only was I happy with warmer weather, but also a posting on the bulletin board brought a smile: Ziemer had been promoted to Private First Class. Good grades and good deportment were paying off. I dove right in, again, and continued to study hard. Five-dollar allowances followed.

I needed the money, too. Since we were residing in south Florida, cadets in good standing were allowed to go to the beach. Oh, the beautiful beaches. And girls in bathing suits. And delicious pizza and submarine sandwiches. And hot cars everywhere. A teenager's dream, twice a week.

Maybe I am a bit crazy, but I would grow to prefer Gainesville over Hollywood. Perhaps because we spent more time in Gainesville. Or because my indoctrination to RMA happened there (sort of like imprinting to a baby duck). I preferred the Gainesville grounds with the Gone-With-The-Wind buildings, soaring pine trees and majestic Lake Lanier.

The Hollywood barracks were just not cozy. I recall concrete floors, concrete hallways and adjoining suites with three to four boys in each of the two rooms.

We also endured constant automobile traffic circling the Hollywood campus. And town boys honking their blasted horns.

But the change of scenery was welcomed, and our time in Hollywood went by quickly. No sooner would we arrive in Hollywood than we were packing up to return to Georgia. The trip back to Gainesville was a superb example of well-coordinated logistics. The academy would load 600 cadets onto 12 busses, and 12 hours later, the chartered caravan would complete the 700-mile jaunt. And yes, there was a bit of celebration on the busses. After all, the school year would be ending in two and a half months.

I continued to study and was rewarded with promotion to corporal shortly after we arrived in Gainesville. At the end of May, I went to California to spend the summer with my family. And work. I held my first "real" job at the age of 14, washing dishes in Myrt's Cafe. She paid the minimum wage, $1.15 per hour. I cashed my paychecks, bought 45rpm records and took Paulette bowling.

What a Difference a Year Makes

When I returned to RMA in the fall of 1963, I began the year as the second or third highest ranking sophomore. As a sergeant first class (SFC), I was charged with a squad of 10 cadets in "E" Company. What does an SFC do? He directs his team leaders and provides training, discipline and mentoring to members of the squad. The promotion was a nice bump up from corporal.

My hard work was paying off. As an SFC in the 10th grade, I was on track to become a senior cadet officer, meaning company commander or higher, providing I could keep my nose to the grindstone. I hit the books even harder. I was proud of what I had accomplished and wanted to keep it going.

At this point, did I like the academy? Among one's peers, it was not "cool" to say you enjoyed academy life. I liked the campus. I liked several teachers and administrators. I had made some good friends, and we enjoyed sharing a few perspectives. We were teenagers, and conversations drifted to girls, sports and cars. A shared disdain for academy life was *expected* of us.

I joined the cross-country team, coached by Colonel Vander Pyl. He was a nice man and one of the few officers who had survived the horrific "Lost Battalion" battle of World War I. I enjoyed running cross country. Over the river and through the Georgia woods we went. The last half mile of the course was an uphill burn, a home-court advantage once a runner got used to it.

The temperature was dropping into the low thirties on November 22, 1963. The terrible date would come to be known as "the day America lost its innocence," when President Kennedy was assassinated. Every cadet and staff member at Riverside was in a state of shock. Some were crying.

On that chilly day, two weeks following my 15th birthday, I cheated on an exam and got caught. I did not need to do it, and I did not know how to do it properly. I remember thinking how clever I was that I could get away with it. Maybe this was the same bug that made me take pictures of the Cuban airport during the biggest lockdown in that nation's history. Cocky and full of myself. Plain stupidity.

Standing at attention in the Commandant's Office, Colonel Engle C. May calmly asked me about it. "Yes sir," I admitted. "I did it." No excuse offered. Col. May issued me a 50-demerit offense, and I was busted down to private. I would walk the Bull Ring for five hours and be ordered to move out of 'E' Company quarters.

I was a pee-on again and living in 'D' Company barracks among strangers. In a flash, everything I had worked for was gone. My predicament was worse than when I had started at Riverside the year before. I had no status then because new cadets start without status. But I had come to be a high-ranking sophomore, who got busted down in front of the battalion.

Though I had acted nonchalantly about my feelings for Riverside, when I lost my status, I realized *then* how much it meant to me. I identified with success, not failure. I needed to fill the void but was in no mood to rise early to study.

The Christmas break came three weeks later, and I went home to spend the holidays with Mom and Paulette. In my state of mental numbness, Christmas was mostly a blur. I did befriend a great cross-country runner, Robin Caldwell, who ran for Barstow High School and broke a few records in the mid-sixties. He was a good friend at a time when I needed one. But in the back of my mind, I knew I had to return to the academy and face my "demons."

Christmas ended, and I returned to the Florida campus. My head was not on straight, and I was staying in hot water and accruing too many demerits. Because I was not studying sufficiently, I was having difficulty in Algebra 2, a progressive subject one must keep up with. I was on my own wavelength, my own private network, and it was a garbled mess.

Consequently, I walked the Bull Ring. Around and around and around I went. Col. May refused to give me sympathy. The man was as tough as they come. He talked to me in a quiet, stern voice and told me that I would have to pull myself out of the mud. "Nobody can do it for you," he explained. Col. May helped me understand actions have consequences and throwing a temper tantrum solves nothing. With piercing blue eyes and without raising his voice, he showed me the abyss, and I did not like what I saw. He made me grow up.

The word "love" is not a term one sees associated with the Commandant's Office of a military academy. But Col. May was the epitome of tough love. Serving as Riverside's Commandant for 33 years, he had his eye on the big picture, the maturity of cadets and their future success. Old-fashioned discipline can lay a rock-solid foundation for maturity and success in adult life. Colonel May lived that mantra and helped many boys to see the light.

So what if I had stumbled? Big deal. Though I hated the negative energy, the "bad vibes," RMA and my brothers-in-blue would lead me to the sunshine. Additional maturity, though, would be required before I would hit full stride.

Back to Good

As Internet and cell phones had not been invented, it was problematic for cadets to stay in touch with the outside world. Thank goodness the Japanese had invented the transistor radio. Many cadets had radios, and we would listen to music after taps. In early 1964, we rocked to a group from Liverpool, The Beatles, who conquered America with their first number one hit, "I Want To Hold Your Hand." A few weeks later, we were captivated by a sporting event in nearby Miami, as a young boxer named Cassius Clay upset Sonny Liston in the heavyweight championship of the world. I can still hear shouts of "I am the greatest" echoing through the Hollywood halls.

Returning to Gainesville in the spring of my sophomore year was a relief, as it signified the school year would be ending shortly. Still in a bit of a funk, Cadet Ziemer was doing a better job of walking the straight and narrow path. I was, however, looking forward to spending the summer in Maracaibo.

Indeed, it was energizing to return to Venezuela, to the comfort of my home, my friends, especially Augusto, and my girlfriend, Irma. Perspective is often gained by stepping away from a situation. The swim clubs of Maracaibo... the delicious food... the contagious music... all helped me to clear my head.

When I returned to Riverside in the fall of 1964 for my junior campaign, I was feeling stronger and ready to carry on. During the course of the year, I would be promoted to sergeant. President Lyndon Johnson came to Gainesville in the fall to deliver a speech on his war on poverty. Cadets lined the streets to see his motorcade pass. The President waved at us, and we saluted him.

Later that year, while in battalion formation on the quad, a furious Colonel May addressed the corps. He had locked down the campus because someone had thrown paint on a faculty officer's car. I remember him stating, "I do not care if your parents are coming. No cadet is leaving this campus until we find out who did this!" Of course, Colonel May always got his man.

In the spring of my junior year, I spent four or five days in the Riverside infirmary with the flu. All I recall from the stay is that the nurse took excellent care of me, and I slept a lot. But there was much going on outside of RMA.

As the 1965 school year ended, the largest anti-Vietnam "teach-in" took place 2,500 miles away from Riverside, at the University of California-Berkeley. Reflecting the two opposing sides of a social divide that would soon tear the country apart, the two top songs of early 1966 were "California Dreamin'" and "Ballad of the Green Berets." Funny thing was... many, if not most, Riverside cadets liked both songs.

My senior year at RMA was a time of celebration. I made the honor roll many times and was promoted to my highest held rank, to master sergeant. I was honored to join the Fusiliers drill team (the academy's premiere showmen) and be awarded an efficiency medal for top performance of military duties. As platoon sergeant of 'D' Company, 3rd Platoon, I reported to a great guy, Lieutenant John Delcambre. "Del" would go on to serve in the US military as a surgeon. He would also be the recipient of three purple hearts.

Even with the passing of several years, wonderful memories of my senior year remain with me. Helping me to reach academic term honors, I had superb teachers, in particular, Major Nichols and Major Wilson ("Goomba.") I had a blast with good friends, Hank Koch, Bruce Mather and Guy Allard. Because Guy was the First Sergeant of "D" Company, we shared the same barracks. We took leave together and visited Clemson University, about 75 miles from Gainesville. Hearts were broken in Clemson. A few of us would also travel to Atlanta to dine at the Little Italy restaurant, by the Greyhound Bus Station, where we could enjoy a Schlitz or two.

During my senior year, I roomed with a nice boy who suffered from epilepsy. He was fine as long as he took medication. With Riverside's hectic schedule, he did miss taking his prescription a few times, and a few grand mal seizures resulted. I did my best to hold him still so that he would not hurt himself. Colonel May thanked me for working with him. I was happy to help the kid, because he always tried his best.

To this day, 60 years after the fact, I am bothered by the mistake I made in my sophomore year. But I believe bouncing back is a most valuable lesson. Throughout my life, whenever I have been down, I have known that nothing can stop me from getting back up. I am not afraid to try and not afraid to fail.

This article is not intended to bring accolades to the writer, but rather to the school, to Riverside Military Academy, for teaching me how to live *properly*. I grew in every way at Riverside. Intellectually. Morally. And yes, physically. I entered the academy at a height of five feet and graduated one foot taller. But physical development is pointless without an elevated sense of mental toughness, intellectual development and personal accountability, which were all acquired at Riverside. By no means was I unique or special. I am sure 95% of four-year boys would say the same.

I was ecstatic that Mom and Paulette attended my graduation ceremonies. When my name was called as winner of the Military Superior Cadet Award, I stood proud and Mom cried.

The last thing I did at Riverside on May 31 was to join the graduation march with fellow cadets. We formed a giant "R" and sang the school's alma mater:

Hail Alma Mater dear
To us be ever near
Give us thy strength to bear
Thy spirit on
When we depart from thee
May we still loyal be
And carry on for thee
Riverside dear

And then, 600 hats were thrown to the sky.

Riverside had an enrollment of 500 boys in 2022. While annual cost to attend RMA is ~$50,000, scholarship assistance may be available.

SHADY LADY OF SHADY LANE

I believe John Denver was spot-on when he wrote, "Death is not an ending, but a symbol of movement along the path upon which we are all traveling. As it may be painful to lose contact with the physical aspect of one we love, the spirit can never be lost. We have been and always will be a part of each other."

Because LaWanda Myree Sjolin is a transcendent part of me, it is an honor and privilege to present her eulogy. My mother demonstrated a mental toughness, an intelligence of wit and an unshakable sense of humor, which allowed her to overcome the possibility of giving up.

LaWanda was born to Dewey and Jewel Gandy in Oklahoma in the early days of the Great Depression. During this difficult era, bread winners did whatever they could to support their families. LaWanda's father drove an 18-wheeler and moved houses when most rural roads were made of dirt. The work was exhausting, and each grueling day brought a new challenge. It was not unusual for Dewey to encounter a bridge half as wide as the house carried upon his trailer.

He could have given up then but he did not. His "Okie ingenuity" found a way to widen the bridge or construct a new one and continue on down the road. LaWanda's life was like that. Obstacles like impassable bridges never stopped her from reaching a destination.

No matter how hard were the times, LaWanda, her older sister Lois, and her two brothers, Paul and Dewey, never went without the essential necessities. Mom would have a new coat in early winter and a pretty dress in the spring. Her brothers were also adept at bagging squirrels for the kitchen pot.

As a member of the Fox High School band, LaWanda won several contests playing the brass cornet. In her senior year, she advanced to the state finals. She took the tournament so seriously that in the evening before the event, she broke out in blotchy, red hives.

She could have given up then but she did not. When her name was called, she strolled on stage, looking like a spotted leopard, with head held high, and played the cornet to the best of her ability.

Never intimidated by a task at hand, LaWanda earned the respect of fellow classmates. In her high school yearbook, one of those students wrote:

> *LaWanda Gandy*
> *Loves a boy in the Navy*
> *With hair blond and wavy*

When the Second World War ended, that boy in the Navy came home, and LaWanda married her childhood sweetheart to become Mrs. Kelly Ziemer. They left Oklahoma in 1947 in an old Plymouth and headed for the sandy pastures of California. They settled in Long Beach with Kelly working in the oil field. I arrived in late 1948 after Mom had spent some 20 hours in labor. She would kid me that it was a miracle she would speak to me after such a painful delivery.

My earliest memories of Mom are of her pulling me to the beach in a little red wagon. After a peanut butter and jelly picnic, she would teach me to swim in the ocean. Little did we know of God's purpose in those lessons.

We moved to Bakersfield in 1952, which marked the beginning of a difficult time in LaWanda's life. First, her oldest brother Paul - whom she adored - was killed in a tragic oil field catastrophe. Then in 1953, Mom was driving Dad to an oil well job when a drunk driver side-swiped their car, causing it to roll several times. Dad was thrown out of the car, pinning him underneath. He was left with a temporarily paralyzed left side, Mom with a broken neck. Like many people in those days, we were without money and insurance.

She could have given up then but she did not. LaWanda recovered, regrouped, re-focused, and in 1956 gave birth to the most wonderful child, Paulette. My baby sister made the family stronger, and the blessing brought a renewed sense of joy and determination.

Two years later, a guardian angel would come to the family's rescue. While swimming in a friend's pool, we failed to notice that Paulette had slipped through her swimming tube. I saw her in the deep end and was able to dive down and bring her to the surface.

When Paulette came out of the water, she was purple, and I will not forget the look of terror on Mom's face. After several panicked revival attempts...

Paulette came back, and the horror on Mom's face was replaced with sobs of gratitude to God that her daughter was again with us.

Paulette, it was Mom that saved you. She taught me how to swim.

Dad found work in Venezuela in 1960 and went there alone to earn money to send for us. While awaiting travel funds, LaWanda's mother, Jewel, only 58 years of age, died of a heart attack. Mom was then without her husband who was oceans away, and mother who had passed to the other world.

Through all of this, Mom worked as a minimum-wage stock clerk at JC Penny's in Bakersfield. She made sure that Paulette and I were well fed, nicely clothed, and that I made it to school on time and did my homework. Her smile and warm word of encouragement were never far away.

LaWanda's wonderful sense of humor carried her through life's many storms. Character can be measured by how well one copes with stormy weather, rather than how bright one sparkles in the sunshine. In the midst of a tornado, she would say, "It doesn't affect me, 'fect me, 'fect me, 'fect me..."

In June of 1961, Dad was able to send funds for our travel from Los Angeles to Venezuela via the lengthy Pan Am turbo-prop route. After a 22-hour flight that touched down in four Central American countries and nearly crashed... after the man behind us had upchucked all over our new travelling clothes... we finally arrived in Maracaibo. As we stepped outside of the customs area, we were excited to see Dad, and Mom was elated that events of the past year were in the rear-view mirror.

LaWanda enjoyed many things in Venezuela. The beaches. The sunsets. The traditional music. Swimming in the warm, crystal-clear Caribbean water. Seated safely on our apartment balcony, we would remain spellbound for hours by God's astonishing all-night show of chain lightning over beautiful Lake Maracaibo. And the tasty local cuisine, the ultimate comfort food, scored high on her list.

On one evening in Maracaibo, Mom, Paulette and I were dining at an Italian restaurant. A middle-aged Latin man, seated directly across the restaurant, was giving Mom the eye. In those days, LaWanda was a beautiful woman. One uncle described her as "Hollywood pretty."

Clearly, the Latin lover forgot what he was doing. While staring at LaWanda, his fork load of spaghetti missed his mouth and speared his nose. The poor fellow was so embarrassed he promptly paid the bill and left the restaurant.

I vividly remember Mom trying to teach me how to dance in our apartment. To Bobby Darin's "Dream Lover," she did her best to show me how to dip, twirl and shuffle. All I can say is, let us pray that I never have to save Paulette by performing dance moves.

Paulette and I were very fortunate to inherit LaWanda's love of melodic music. You should have heard her wail on the piano and sing big-band hits of the 40's, such as "Sentimental Journey" and "(Somewhere) Over The Rainbow." Doris Day and Ray Charles were among her favorites. Elvis, too.

Mom left Venezuela with Paulette in late 1962 because "things" were just not working out. Without a doubt, Kelly and LaWanda truly loved each other. No blame to cast, but if we must, alcohol was the guilty party. And so, LaWanda was then on her own, divorced from her high-school sweetheart, with her 13-year-old son far away in a Georgia military school, and with her five-year-old daughter under doctor's care for chronic asthma.

She could have given up then but she did not. LaWanda landed in Barstow, California, where she could depend on the assistance of her loving father, Dewey, and where she could in turn help him. Paulette was enrolled in the first grade, and Mom found employment at a local drug store as a stock clerk and sales assistant. Barstow's desert climate helped to alleviate Paulette's asthma. In a few months, LaWanda had bounced back. The woman could not be kept down.

Twenty years after LaWanda had left Oklahoma in a raggedy, old Plymouth, she would marry a man who sold new ones. She tied the knot in 1964 with Vernon Sjolin, owner of a very successful Chrysler / Plymouth dealership. "Vern" proved to be a good husband, as well as a second dad to Paulette. LaWanda and Vern worked hard and enjoyed a nice living for a few years.

But in 1967, the Barstow bank, then in financial trouble, abruptly called in Vern's loan against his consignment of new inventory; and consequently... they lost the business. Two years later, LaWanda and Vern would divorce, as the marriage could not recover from the crushing loss of their company.

She could have given up then but she did not. Seeking a change of scenery, Mom and Paulette moved to San Diego, where LaWanda found work with the La Jolla newspaper. Paulette was in the sixth grade, and I had been drafted into the Army. What did LaWanda do next? She had a two-story tree house built in her back yard, where she could enjoy warm sunsets and cold martinis. On the front page of the *Daily Californian* newspaper, LaWanda was quoted: "Well, honey, I'm from Oklahoma. We just always had treehouses back there."

Within the year, LaWanda would arrange purchase of the El Cajon Motel. With motel ownership, comes a never-ending stream of work and sleepless nights, but Mom, with Paulette's help, was able to carve out a decent living.

Many wonderful things happened during this era. Paulette met Pastor Tom McAloon, was introduced to Calvary Ranch and became a reborn Christian. LaWanda's grandsons - Donovan, Jamie and Kris - were born to parents Joe and Pat. Paulette became Mrs. McAloon, and LaWanda returned to Barstow to own and operate the Shady Lane Recreational Vehicle Park.

Mom single-handedly operated this RV park, which like motel work, is a 24/7 obligation. She utilized a shiny, pink golf cart to zip around the lot quickly. On the back of the cart was a sign that read, "Shady Lady of Shady Lane."

Hundreds of LaWanda's park and motel guests were repeat customers. They returned to the Shady Lady's retreat time and time again, as they could count on her spotless housekeeping, her friendly and sincere service, and of course, her unique sense of humor.

LaWanda moved to Las Vegas in 1982 to retire and be closer to Lucille, her best friend from the Bakersfield days. Shortly thereafter, her youngest grandson, Joey, was born to Joe and Roxanne, and was followed a few years later by her only granddaughter, Megan. LaWanda loved all of her grand-children deeply, and in spite of illness and hardships, she rarely missed a birthday or special occasion.

Though LaWanda had her demons, she made the best of her situation. She would agree that if you are not busy living, then you are busy dying. The greatest manifestation of wisdom is humility, and she sang that song every day. To her, the biggest sin is committed by the individual who would waste a life, who would not fight back, who would not do his or her best.

Her favorite book was the dictionary. She would read it for hours. When she came across a word that fascinated her, she would tell me about it.

In her later years, LaWanda insisted on living alone, so she would not be a "burden" to her children. Paulette and I would have gladly taken her in, and we offered family care and accommodation many times. In the end, Mom put (what she saw as) the welfare of her children above her own. But my business would not exist today without her assistance; and likewise, Calvary Ranch would not have become a pillar of hope without her help.

Cancer came in 1997, and it was all too swift. She could have given up then but she did not. Rising above her final pain, on her hospital deathbed, she again triumphed by finding the strength to say to her children her last words, "I love you."

~~~~~~

To LaWanda, the biggest sin is committed by the individual who would waste a life... who would not fight back... who would not do his or her best.

BE ALL YOU CAN BE

As a youngster, I thought I was pretty clever. That I could be whatever I desired, and sail wherever I wished. Influence most anything.

The older I become... the more I realize... the less I control.

Is this metamorphosis brought on by a dimming of the light or realization of the truth? The former is self-explanatory. And as far as the truth goes, God gives us free will to be able to see the truth. He gives us an abundance of rope to hang ourselves or lasso the moon.

Whereas leashes vary in length, the US Army nailed it with their TV slogan, "Be all you *can* be." In that often-misinterpreted motto, a largely neglected meaning of *can* is "be permitted to." Likewise, Proverbs 16:9 of the Bible reads, "The heart of man plans his way, but the Lord establishes his steps."

Bearing in mind the varying capacities of men, we are not equal in our abilities to plan our ways. While we are all made of the same stuff, we are packaged with enormous differences in our wills. Some men can scarcely conceptualize an idea, while others can create a complex design. One man plans to become CEO, while another man sets his sights on being an electrician.

The Bible teaches us that every person has free will to choose *(my words: as much as he can)* his own path, and whether the choice is for janitor or chairman of the board... if he is righteous... "The Lord establishes his steps." This fundamental teaching is expanded by King Solomon in Proverbs 3:6: "In all your ways acknowledge Him / And He shall direct your paths."

In other words, when we (whoever we are) trust in the Lord and acknowledge Him as much as we can, when we are all in, God will move mountains for us. We have temporal will to decide what we will do and embark on that course; however, *perpetual* victory depends on our relationship with God.

But man does not have to acknowledge God in order to reach a worldly port of call. Even though extremely sinful individuals do not have a relationship with God, the fact remains that they have free will to head north or south.

Throughout the journey, they are on their own; the Lord does not establish steps or direct paths of terrible people committing devilish acts. Which leads to the burning question, why does a loving God let men commit atrocities? Because man can exercise free will, and God works through suffering to draw us to Himself. Because Revelation 7:15-17 tells us that heaven is filled with peace, joy and praise, eternally. And in the end, what becomes of the evil perpetrators is answered in Proverbs 16:4: "The Lord has made everything for its purpose... even the wicked for the day of trouble." In other words, God's final judgment on the wicked looms large. So evil doers can get their way here and now, but ultimately, they will not.

This ability to call our own shots applies to third-dimension stuff in the physical universe. If we could will our way in time, perhaps we would have unrestricted free will. Channeling through time though is exclusively reserved for God. As Jesus says, "I am the Alpha and the Omega, the Beginning and the End... who is and who was and who is to come..." (Revelation 1:8)

Christians know that while gravity and sin hold them down on terra firma, the Spirit lifts them up. John Kennedy understood the concept of spiritual gravity at an early age. A powerful yet humble man, he reached a position regarded as the pinnacle of human achievement. Still, on his Oval Office desk was a sign that read, "Oh God, thy ocean is so great and my ship is so small."

God gives us free will to select a destination. When we acknowledge Him in all our ways, our ship becomes mighty. But all vessels, no matter how mighty, encounter torrential storms. Everybody endures pain, regret and heartbreak. And when hearts are down, it can be tough to focus on the horizon and stay the course. In my case, the loss of loved ones has been hard to deal with, but time after time, God has helped me to see clearly and navigate life's seas.

Throughout the fleeting voyage, we are charmed by a fête of must-have stuff. Material trappings on earth is a great illusion; the stuff evaporates so quickly. Yet, as the ultimate example of idol worship, several scholarly types embrace vaporous stuff, *in itself*, as the origin of it all. Interaction of primordial gases, these freethinkers say, caused one great Big Bang, which by minute chance, led to perfect conditions for the creation of you, me and Pamela's pet poodle.

Fred Hoyle, a famous mathematician, said, "The chance that higher life forms emerged by chance is comparable with the chance that a tornado sweeping through a junkyard might assemble a Boeing 747 from materials therein."

The scientific community mostly agree that there was a gaseous Big Bang, yet I remain hung up on the basic question, where did the gas come from?

Just as hot air rises, cynics and doubters abound and their voices can be loud. John Lennon made a statement in 1966 that rocked the planet, "The Beatles," he declared, "are more popular than Jesus." Jumping on the bandwagon just one month later, *Time* magazine published an article, asking, "Is God Dead?" The Beatles had a massive following. So did *Time*. Lennon's brash (though misconstrued) words and *Time's* blatant, money-making headline added fuel to the eternal fire. The debate was on.

That age-old debate, *if God exists as our creator and salvation*, continues. More so now than ever, we are a world divided. So many troupes of intolerant followers are riding their own white horses, surfing their own rogue waves. Muslims and Christians. Communists and capitalists. Republicans and Democrats. Homosexuals and heterosexuals. Jesus freaks and atheists. Separation by what we believe in has become not only extreme, but the norm. Whichever side one is on is ABSOLUTELY RIGHT, and the other side is not just wrong... but STUPID.

On such an emotionally charged stage, it is difficult to discuss differences with the other side. Our chosen leaders are unwilling to find common ground. Compromise, the major instrument of working democracy, has been replaced with disdain and disagreement. We do not have to travel to Washington to witness this ugliness. Many of us are exactly the same with our neighbors. In a free society, for the most part, representatives reflect their constituents.

Unfortunately, we have dug ourselves into a pretty deep hole down here. Jesus told us to love Him and to love others, and too many of us have failed. But what of the testimony that He died for our sins? Why would He do that? The answer is simple. Jesus the Creator of everything is our loving Father. He did for all of us what any father should do for his child. I would gladly take my daughter's Crohn's disease. This is what a good father does.

Why then are there so many insistent nonbelievers? The underlying reason atheists are so adamant might be because God is actively pursuing them. They are too busy justifying their own cynicism to consider other possibilities, plus a puffed-up ego will not admit there is anything greater than himself. While theistic denial is an obvious way to disregard one's own sin, I believe there are no atheists present on an airplane going down.

The author's explanation for denying God does not necessarily apply to the terribly downtrodden. We should empathize with "down-and-out" folks who are homeless, chronically ill, severely injured, physically or sexually abused… It is understandable that demoralized individuals could have their doubts. But Jesus did say, "Blessed are the poor in spirit, For theirs is the kingdom. Blessed are those who mourn, For they shall be comforted." (Matthew 5:3-4) And He also stated, "If you can believe, all things *are* possible to him who believes." (Mark 9:23)

All In

In my experience, as I clean up my own act, I feel distinctly closer to the Lord. When I screw up, I find it hard to face Him. This is all spelled out in the Bible, the User's Manual on how to live our lives. Indeed, there is a right way and a wrong way, and we have free will to chart a course to the north or south.

It is nearly impossible to find something when one is looking the wrong way. Jeremiah 29:13 tells us how to find the Lord: "You will seek Me and find Me when you search for Me with all your heart." The scripture also explains why one will not find the Lord. To be clear, dilettantes will not succeed. Practicing what they preach by helping others to find the Lord, my sister Paulette and son Kris have spent thousands of hours in their churches, doing what they can to help the hungry, the needy, the addicted, the children.

I found the Lord one dim night in 1992. On my knees. Twelve hours pleading. Begging for mercy I did not deserve. Crying out to God to end my addiction, I recited Proverbs 3:5-6 over and over and over:

> *Trust in the Lord with all your heart*
> *And lean not on your own understanding*
> *In all your ways acknowledge Him*
> *And He will make your paths straight*

On that gloomy night, I learned we do not have to be inside a church to say, "Trust in the Lord." Why not? Because communion with God is a spiritual wavelength, and as the morning sun lit up my room, I knew my cries had been heard. Jesus answered my prayer and freed me from alcohol enslavement. He removed the craving from my brain, that uncontrollable, evil screaming, and He also deleted my pack-a-day need for cigarettes. I was *instantly* cured without any pain of withdrawal. The marvel that Jesus performed in my life is comparable to His New Testament miracles, as documented by the apostles.

How does one find the Prince of Peace? James, a man history records as the brother of Jesus, tells us if we draw near to God, He draws near to us. Laying everything on the line, I found God when I made the choice to search for Him with all of my heart. And when we do find Him, what does He offer? To free people from habits of sin and to give people a more abundant life. Ultimately, to offer them eternal life in heaven.

Imagine a heaven of indescribable beauty. Without pain. Without heartbreak. John, one of the twelve apostles, wrote in Revelation 21:4, "God will wipe away every tear from their eyes; there shall be no more death, nor sorrow, nor crying. There shall be no more pain..." For two millennia, countless skeptics have attempted to negate this sacred message of hope, by asking, "Where is the proof?"

By radiating the peace of a spiritual bond with Christ, I believe the proof is in the eyes of the believer, from knowing one's steps are being directed by Him. I do not get this same exuberant sense of eternal salvation from my car or stamp collection. Romans 5:1 says, "Therefore, having been justified by faith, we have peace with God through our Lord Jesus Christ."

To know something is real - that it actually exists - we do not have to see it. Though we cannot see the wind, we can feel it, and we can see its effect, bending trees, scattering leaves. We cannot see love, but we know its effect, a mother comforting her child, kissing her husband. We may not see God, but we can experience His presence in the wind blowing, His love spreading and lost souls being saved in the middle of the night.

Cynics and doubters have claimed for 2,000 years believers have been duped by the greatest hoax in history, that the scriptural account of Jesus is a lie. But if Christ rose from the dead, that triumph trumps all. Meanwhile, we are free to choose which story we wish to believe. Everything or nothing.

Be still and close your eyes - or perhaps open your eyes - and try to envision for just one moment that this God story is true. What if John 3:16 is truthful, that, "God so loved the world that He gave His only begotten Son... that whoever believes in Him should not perish but have everlasting life."

Are you prepared to risk your personal eternity by not believing?

Not me. I am all in.

Bullets bullets everywhere
Nor any thought to think

EXCURSION

Vignettes of love for friends, a child, a woman and above all, God. Also…trains, poetry, Las Vegas, boating, briefcases, Butler, Beatles and Joan Baez.

THE TRAIN

When I was a small boy, Dad would take me to the Bakersfield train station, where I would board the Santa Fe Special. I loved those summer journeys to visit my grandparents in Barstow, a sleepy town in the Mojave Desert.

As I traveled alone, Dad would slip the conductor five bucks to keep an eye on me. The conductor was an old Black gentleman who looked like John Coffey from the movie, *The Green Mile*, and he called me "Mister Joe." Running up and down the octave scale, the giant would greet me in a glorious voice, and his greeting sounded like a gospel song: "Mister Joe, welcome on my train. It's real good to see you, son. I got a special seat just for you."

God, it was exciting. The train was just so big and powerful and noisy. To a small boy of six, boarding the beast was like jumping into the mouth of a mythical creature. And when the iron horse was ready to roll, he would start to snort. Slowly at first. And then hissing. Calmly. Mightily.

As he worked up a full head of steam, the steel stallion would begin snorting faster. I feared he might explode. I mean nobody's heart can beat that fast! And when he got to running flat out, Lord my God Almighty... RIKETY-RIKETY-RAK, RIKETY-RIKETY-RAK... He would blow his stack and the steam would go a mile high. And then he would scream!

And I loved it. Flying down the tracks... going a million miles per hour... nothing could stop the train! CHOOOOOOO! CHOOOOOOOOOOOOOOOOO! Folks could hear the metal monster whistle for miles, an incredible sound, something of a cross between a dinosaur's yell and a chorus of pan pipes.

Everybody in town heard the whistle and it told them there was a way out. Nothing could stop the train.

~~~~~~

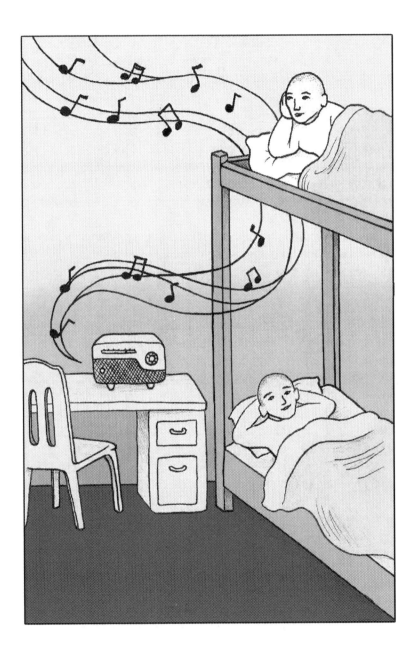

THE BEATLES

Lying in my bunk at Riverside Military Academy, listening to the radio, I could not believe how perfect the song sounded. "I Want To Hold Your Hand" was the first number one hit by the four lads of Liverpool, and the tightness of the 1964 rocker convinced me The Beatles had been practicing for years. In fact, by the time they had this first burst of success in America, they had performed live some 1,200 times, primarily to tough crowds in Hamburg, Germany.

And so, when America first heard The Beatles, they were refined. So together and harmonious, the lads had to be on the same wavelength to create such a seamless blending of lyrics and melody. Every guitar lick, every drum roll, every soaring vocal note in "I Want To Hold Your Hand" is complementary.

The Beatles were not imitators of anything or anybody. Like Bob Dylan and Mickey Newbury, they were the real deal... with their own words and music and standards. But unlike Dylan and Newbury, they were rock/pop artists; and so, their songs would reach the masses in all four corners of the planet. The group would disband in 1970, leaving fans with many magnificent albums jam-packed with melodic and relevant masterpieces.

The impact has continued. In the 70's and 80's, my work in the broadcast industry took me to over 100 countries. From China to Uruguay, I heard Beatles music... in the airports... in the taxicabs... in the restaurants.... Though my travels happened before the Internet was a "thing," the good news had spread like wildfire. The joyful sound of The Beatles was everywhere.

Even at the Vatican. In 2010, Pope Benedict XVI compiled a list of his top ten rock albums. *Revolver* topped the Pontiff's chart. Closer to home, everybody in my family enjoys The Beatles. Dad loved "Hey Jude," and Mom liked many of their melodies. Wife Roxanne, a dancer, moves to "Day Tripper," and sister Paulette rocks to early Beatles. My children, born between 1972 and 1988, have their favorites: Jamie grooves to "Yellow Submarine," while Kris sings "Hey Jude." Joey and Megan are fans of most of the group's oeuvre, while Taylor fancies "Let It Be." And now, the grandkids are crooning their tunes.

The Beatles have bestowed an abundance of joy on the weary world and have helped us to connect. Indeed, it is easier for people to be on the same page when they sing the same song. My five generations of warblers would agree.

SITTING BACKWARDS ON A TRAIN

As fortune would have it, Sunday, March 8, 2009 was a free day. So, I hopped a train in Amsterdam and headed north. I was going up to Drenthe Country to visit a good friend. Egbert Meijers was birthing another album (his sixth), and my visit was falling on the same day as the CD release party. Waiting by track 14B at Centraal Station, I asked a tall, mustached man if the next train would go to Assen.

"I hope so," he quipped. "I'm driving it."
"Well then," I said, "I will be in good hands."
"Don't be so sure about that," he cautioned. "Next week they're sending me in for psychological evaluation."
"Oh," I replied taking a few steps back.
"I'm just kidding," he exclaimed. "Hah hah hah! Boy, I had you going!"

Truth be known, the engineer did get me going. It was early in the morning, and I needed a coffee fix. Anyway, when he asked why I was traveling to Assen, I explained I was off to visit a friend. "Wonderful," he said. "That is why I love my job!"

The silver train pulled in exactly on time on track 14B. Stepping into the car, I selected a window seat facing backwards towards the caboose. I love sitting backwards on a speeding train, listening to Mickey Newbury on my iPod and watching the present disappear.

I sat there enjoying my music and the past, and then, like a sledgehammer, it hit me. I blew it. In the sixties, like so many others, I thought we would change the world. We did not. People are still fighting. People are broke. Mother Nature is under the weather like never before. Totally blameless, my children are inheriting a sick planet. "I am sorry," said I to the window.

As I dropped into a meditative state, the train flew down the tracks. Two hours later, we arrived in Assen, right on time. Egbert met me at the station and we hugged (you know, in a manly way). "Welcome, Joe! God, it's good to have you here!" With Egbert's sincere embrace, my woe for the future dissolved, temporarily, though that quickly.

I had met Egbert five years earlier at a Newbury gathering in Austin, Texas. Straight away, I could sense intelligence by the way the guy carried himself. This is a person who has loved, laughed and cried. Indeed, when he sang, he did cry. The older I become, the more I appreciate a soulman who has the strength to shed tears. We hit it off immediately. I felt at home in his company and was happy to be with him again. On his own turf.

We jumped into his car, and Egbert told me we would go directly to RTV Drenthe Radio, where he was scheduled for an on-air interview to discuss the new album. At the station, I downed two cups of strong coffee, while we awaited Egbert's appearance on Podium 30.

Egbert had worked for the FM station four years earlier, serving as editor and producer and creating the format for the Podium 30 program. The show was now hosted by Lukas Koops, who interviewed Egbert for at least an hour. As I do not speak Drents, I cannot comment on content, but judging from the vocal tones, sparkling eyes and contented smiles... the session went well.

Afterwards, Egbert said we had time for a quick tour. He drove to Grolloo, a small community with a population of 500, to show me the quaint farmhouse where he had grown up. Many houses in the area are over 200 years old. Charming storybook cottages with thatch roofs. Where Egbert acquired his sincerity is clear; it would be problematic to be a bullshitter in a tiny village. Before departing Grolloo, he pointed out the renowned, one-hundred-year-old café Hofsteenge, a picturesque place where famous artists have played, and where his CD release party would happen in a few hours.

We drove to Egbert's cozy home in Gasselte. I met his wife, Ina, and their beautiful nine-year old daughter, Annerieke. While we enjoyed a tasty meal, I told Egbert he is a lucky man. "Married way over my head," he explained.

As time for rehearsal was drawing near, we packed up the car and drove to Grolloo. When we entered the Hofsteenge, the eight-member band was setting up. This group who plays on the album is a collection of superb musicians, consisting of Kees Hendriks, Peter Deiman, Richard Zoer, Paul van Vlodrop, Ronnie Snippe, Erwin Budike, Joost van Es and Johan Jansen. Friendly guys who take their music seriously.

After the band had rehearsed for an hour or so, many people started to arrive. A long ticket line formed, and folks rushed in to claim the best of the seats.

The room was soon packed, with 400 people crowding into the historic venue. The place was filled with the sound of friends greeting friends and laughter. Until Egbert Meijers and band begin to play. Then the place got quiet.

As the music flowed, the audience reacted with hand clapping, foot stomping, and synchronized swaying. Immediately following the emotional concert, Ina, Annerieke and I helped out at the sales counter. People were snatching up Egbert's albums like piranhas in a feeding frenzy.

Characteristic of one who grew up in a connected village, where many people are on the same communal wavelength, Egbert cares for friends, and the flow is returned. I witnessed numerous showers of affection at the Hofsteenge. As one solemn example, the album is dedicated to his good friend, Ab Gritter, who had unexpectedly passed away a few months earlier.

Though all 14 songs are presented in the Drents language, one does not have to understand the words to feel the passion, which is expressed melodically through blues, ballads, mountain music and rock and roll. The band cooks on an assortment of instruments, including banjo, piano, accordion, mandolin, harmonica, harmonium... as well as steel, acoustic and electric guitars. Indeed, Egbert Meijers is Drents-Dutch, but he is an Americana artist.

The album is titled *Hondsrug Sessies* after the Tom Waits song, "San Diego Serenade," which Egbert translates to Drents as "Hondsrug Serenaode." Songs are included from American songwriter Jimmy Lafave and Swedish songwriter Ulf Lundell. The remaining 11 compositions are all written and arranged by Egbert.

Keeping it real, Egbert does a good job of conveying landscapes of the past. The themes are mostly autobiographical and span several subjects. Lyrics deal with a variety of loves: unrealized love, love for his wife Ina, love for his hometown and province, love for his Drenthe ancestors of 5,000 years ago and love for the true meaning of Christmas.

Several adult themes are confronted, such as self-discovery, the pain of forced retirement and accepting responsibility for the shape of the world. Egbert included an upbeat beer-drinking song, "Verzopen Amsterdammer," which is done in the old Amsterdam beer-hall style. (This ditty is definitely autobiographical!) After paying a visit to Ground Zero in New York City, Egbert wrote the concluding pillar, "Genog Is Genog" ("Enough Is Enough").

The song questions America's emotional reaction after the 9/11 tragedy, by sending B52 bombers instead of a delegation of peacemakers.

This is a great album, a heartfelt and intelligent offering from a connected guy, a responsible soul who takes time to survey the past. The music warms me and makes me feel good about myself.

After the public had departed, we dined on delicious schnitzel and fries. All too soon, it was time to say goodbye. (I hate that part.) Frans Többen drove me to the Assen train station, making the 15-minute drive in nine minutes. As I boarded the Amsterdam Special, I was hoping my psycho-engineer buddy was at the wheel.

I also thought I might find a seat facing forward.

~~~~~~

ANAM CARA

Alexis was 6,000 miles away from home. Out of the blue, Kashi felt that he needed help. She phoned him. "I am sick," Alexis whispered to his wife.

Many of us have experienced a sudden feeling of concern for a loved one who is not physically present, whether he is oceans away or in the next room. It is amazing how often such feelings turn out to reflect reality. The Celts refer to this occurrence as "anam cara." Neuroscientists call it "brain coupling." Psychologists call it "telepathic love," and laymen think of it as a "sixth sense."

While peering into people's brains with fMRI machines, Princeton University neuroscientist Uri Hasson found that when two people profoundly connect... when we relate to another person on a deep level... the activity in our brains mirrors theirs. Even more intriguing, the stronger the connection between two people, the more they "click," and the more the brain scans mirror each other. This mind-melding between "kindred spirits," where brains start working in sync, has been verified in independent studies by researchers from UCLA, Dartsmouth and the University of Technology in Sydney.

Psychologists have long known that some couples begin to think like each other, allowing them to know what their partner is feeling or about to say. During this state, the part of each person's brain that controls the nervous system begins *to beat together*. At this point, when couples are literally on the same wavelength, they can often read each other's minds to some extent.

Surfing the same wave with another soul is an exalted feeling of pure bliss, a blessed joie de vivre. As Richard Bach wrote, "Our soulmate is the one who makes life come to life." I prefer the Gaelic term, "anam cara," which translates to "soul friend," one with whom we can read each other's hearts... the kind of camaraderie that affords comfortable communication.

After basic necessities such as food and shelter, effective communication is paramount. It leads to understanding, to tolerance and on to the possibility of agreement. Our world is so divided now, and disagreement between people is a universal issue. Imagine if wavelength skills could be amplified to a higher level; we could conceivably blow the doors off communication as we know it. Perhaps this is the sort of thing Einstein had in mind when he wrote, "Imagination is more important than knowledge."

HAIKUS WITH A TWIST

Cross a piranha
With a peacock and presto
A politician

~

Lying in state I
See that everybody goes
Around and around

~

Hip hop performed while
Outfitted like a mummy
It's called wrap music

~

Dining on frog legs
My lover toad me frogs at
Peace are them that croak

~

Beginning to end
And back again everything
Here is connected

~

Bodies around souls
Cities wrapped around bodies
Serving one to life

~

He hitched the wagon
To a star overlooking
Starlight outlasts stars

~

We don't die darlin'
Another river empties
Into the ocean

Woman tries to change
Man who wants woman unchanged
While both fight their fates

~

I am not myself
Today but then yesterday
Was once tomorrow

~

Narcissist in love
With his own mythology
Aphrodite weeps

~

When we see the light
The star is no longer there
Twinkling white specter

~

Numero Uno
Sweet LaWanda do you know
You're the one for me

~

I skipped a small stone
Thirteen-thousand years later
A tsunami struck

~

Trust me for a spell
We'll spin this planet princess
Create our own time

~

Be patient my child
The future's a line away
You're already there

~

Met a girl named Ku
And didn't know what to do
I just said haiku

I WOULD GIVE IT ALL

In a panicked rush we arrive
Sirens blasting red lights flashing
Doubled over in screaming pain
My Megan the one who never whines

Hospital hallway winding and wide
While wandering around and around
Code Blue shouts the speaker
A slap in the face that ceiling doors
Open up out of this place

Needle nurses and beeping machines
Snaking IV's dripping drazine
As doctors try to keep us here
God simply tries to make us hear

Spirit connecting sweet eyes reflecting
Agony beyond belief
To see my child suffer this way is
Heartache beyond relief

And I would gladly take your place
Take all your pain away
I would give it all to see you smile
I would gladly take your place

My child you mean more to me
Than me and all that is mine
I would give it all to see you smile
Lord let me take her place

~~~

Megan could have given up then, but she did not.
She turned pain into empathy and became a registered nurse.

THERE SHE STOOD

There she stood with eyes so sweet
To brighten up the night
When she turned and looked my way
I could not tell a lie

She touched the soft spot in my soul
Where very few have gone
I saw her for a second
I have known her for all time

Sure we could have been lovers
We have been eternal friends
I saw her for a second
I have known her for all time

The sun will rise to end the night
The earth will spin away
Her memory will stay with me
Long after I must leave

~~~

YOU HERE ME THERE

You here me there I
Watch you bathing
In the clear water
We share as we tie up
On different sides of
The lake we breathe in
The same sweet air
It keeps us moving
To each other

~~~

Your disguise is complete
When your perfume is all I can see

THE LITTLE COLLEGE THAT COULD

Author's note: As Roxanne and I had become avid fans of Butler's basketball program, I was delighted to write this article in 2011. We were, however, even happier that our son Joey graduated from Butler with academic honors and as President of Butler's "Dawg Pound."

Several colleges have huge basketball budgets. Due to dissimilar methods of bookkeeping, an apples-to-apples comparison is problematic. But Duke appears to have the highest annual budget of all 350 Division I schools, by a factor of at least seven times over Butler University.

Still, Butler is one of only three Division I schools to win at least 25 basketball games in each of the last four seasons, and Butler has advanced to post-season tournament play in nine of the past 14 years. With miniscule budget and only 4,500 students, how does the little school do it?

The Butler Bulldogs are widely known for their toughness, connectedness (a wavelength thing), poise under pressure, spectacular defensive play and extremely high basketball IQ. "The Butler Way" emphasizes these qualities. Not about ego or money. Only about making your teammates better and doing things on and off the court the right way.

In Butler's run through the 2010 tournament - with a team that started three sophomores - they defeated Syracuse (# 1 seed), Kansas State (# 2 seed) and Michigan State (# 5 seed). Winning these games, arguably the toughest test any team had to face, earned Butler the privilege to play the Duke Blue Devils in the final match. That championship game would feature 15 lead changes, and neither team would lead by more than six points. The contest would go down to the last second with Butler coming up one possession short.

President Obama, a baller himself, telephoned the Dawgs to congratulate them on finishing second in the nation. Additionally, this small Indianapolis college fielded two *academic* All Americans on that national runner-up squad. The other three teams in the Final Four? Zip.

What is more impressive than Butler's 2010 run to the title game as a 5 seed? Another trip to the title game in the following year as an 8 seed! In 2011, Butler again advanced to the final game and finished second in the nation. These runs may stand as the greatest accomplishment in all of college sports.

SAD EYED LADY

As Kris Kristofferson was booked to perform at the Greek Theater in Berkeley, I leapt at the opportunity to see him live. The 1976 concert was being billed as a fund-raiser for Caesar Chavez and the United Farm Workers. Not only would I contribute to a good cause, but also, I would see a superb songwriter.

Kristofferson's sensitive songs, such as "Sunday Mornin' Coming Down," had stunned me, while his music smacked of another composer, Mickey Newbury. By penning melodic, *introspective* songs in the country genre in the early 70's, the two Texas troubadours had turned country music on its head. And so, I was excited to experience Kristofferson in person.

But there was another treasure to be revealed at the theater. Before the show began, a friend pointed to a dark-haired woman seated a few rows below. "See the sad-eyed lady in the lowlands. That, my friend, is Joan Baez, and the woman on her right... Mimi Farina."

Without offering an excuse for my livewire reaction, I went straight to Joan and introduced myself. "Hello, Joe," she responded. "I am glad to meet you."

We talked up several topics, including the work I was doing for the Office of Veterans on the UC Davis campus. I explained that my job involved recruiting educationally disadvantaged Vietnam veterans for a gratis study program, which enabled them to earn a GED diploma. "It's pretty hard," I whispered.

"I know it is," she answered. "I am against war, but I support our veterans."

We talked for 15 minutes, and I was impressed with the soft-spoken lady. She referred me to the *Pentagon Papers*, the DOD history of US involvement in Vietnam, released to the *New York Times* by Daniel Ellsberg.

As Kristofferson took the stage, I knew it was time to say goodbye. Offering my hand for a farewell handshake, she held it softly and kissed it. As I looked into her eyes, she said, "God bless you for helping our veterans."

Oh, and by the way, Kristofferson was marvelous.

~~~~~~

BRIEFCASE BLUES

The year was 1980. The place, Montevideo. I was an Area Sales Manager for Harris Broadcast and in Uruguay to make a presentation to the government.

South America's best-kept secret, Uruguay, is tucked away between its giant neighbors, Brazil and Argentina. With hundreds of miles of pristine coastline, Uruguay has stunning beaches of fine, white sand and turquoise water. There you will find 17th century colonial architecture, authentic Gaucho cowboys, mint-condition antique cars, and (many say) the world's most tender beef. And the people? With a laid-back manner, Uruguayans wear big smiles and are super friendly and accommodating. Spending time in the small country was always a blessed relief, especially after fencing with the slick Porteños of bustling Buenos Aires just across the river.

As always, I was in Uruguay to work. The civilian-military regime had decided to procure a high-power television transmitter and antenna system for their national TV network, "Canal 5 Sodre." The turnkey job would be decided by public bid, and offers were expected from worldwide competitors. Therefore, I was glad to be working with our firm's local partner, Juan Arroyo. With Juan, we had already supplied several AM stations and the nation's first FM station. I am not boasting, just setting the stage for what follows.

Juan had arranged our initial appointment with the Director General of Sodre, a position just two notches away from Uruguay's President. As we entered the Director's office, we took our seats in front of his massive desk. Juan said, "Mister Director, the US factory expert, Joe Ziemer, is here to help Sodre solve all of its technical problems in order to realize this important project." The Director General looked at me and asked me for my business card.

I laid my heavy Samsonite briefcase in my lap, opened it and removed a card. When I closed it, I failed to notice the end of my tie was firmly locked inside. As I set the briefcase on the floor, my head went with it. The Director General started laughing, and his laughter went on until the man was gasping for air. Every time I attempted to speak, his uncontrollable laughter would take over. Finally, after about 20 minutes, as Juan and I were leaving, while the Director's head was on his desk, we heard him shout, "Peter Sellers!"

Evidently, we connected with the Director. Four months later, he told us the job was ours... as compensation for the "best floor show" he had ever seen.

ANCHORS AWEIGH

My wife Roxanne and I spent the day boating on Geist Lake in Indianapolis a few years ago. With us were Lola, Judy and Taylor, respectively Roxanne's mom, sister and niece. I enjoyed those peaceful outings. As Captain of the vessel, I sat in the Captain's chair, wore a Captain's hat and insisted that the crew addressed me as - you guessed it - "Captain."

While navigating the waters, a few things pleased the Captain. I enjoyed barking out nonsensical orders, such as "gavel down the jimmy" and "rappel the c-bit." When it was time for lunch, I spouted, "Three bells." The Captain's mess then had to be served within 30 seconds.

Midway through our Sunday voyage, Lola petitioned the Captain for some fishing time. As the Captain wished to please his mother-in-law, the request was granted, and the Captain directed the pontoon into a small cove.

Because the vessel was drifting, the Captain commanded 14-year-old Taylor to secure the anchor. Taylor opened the storage bin and tied the line to a crossbar. "Heave the anchor" was the Captain's subsequent command.

But the anchor was heavy, 75 pounds or so, and Taylor could not handle it. So, the Captain exited the Captain's chair to assist the young swab. "Observe," said the Captain as he tossed the weighty mud hook. As the craft was drifting too close to shore on port side, the Captain heaved the anchor a mighty five meters to starboard.

As all hands watched the anchor disappear into the depths, Captain and crew gasped in horror as the end of the rope followed the anchor down to the bottom. There had been two sections of rope in the storage bin, and the section tied to the boat was not connected to the anchor.

Anchor's away!

~~~~~~

LUCILLE

Lucille arrived shortly after the third hour. She left her pocketbook on the kitchen table and went to the back room. The boy emerged from the shadows and removed an Abraham. He hid the bill in a bag of tasty caramels. The doe-eyed dilettante denied the deed. Three times he would deny the truth. Without the five-spot, Lucille was unable to gas up her glass-topped Montclair. Mercury began rising.

~~~~~~

Kiss o' the witches
Ignorance is bliss I guess
Shakespeare in stiches

~~~~~~

JULIET'S PRAYER

Dear God give us thy strength
To outlive this story's length
Our passion is too far out of control

LOW-LEVEL WAVELENGTH

The television commercial shows two twenty-something women in the ladies' room changing their look. One transforms into a blonde, the other a redhead. Giggling, they leave the room and head out to the excitement of a casino. What they do next is left to the imagination.

Many of us have been there before. History books are filled with accounts of individuals and societies being charmed by the razzle-dazzle of bright lights, pretty people and the allure of a Pied Piper's flute. In the case of Las Vegas, the silver flute comes in the guise of a slick slogan: "What happens in Vegas... stays in Vegas."

The agency that developed the Madison Avenue glitz in 2003, R&R Partners, stated they wanted to convey the feeling of freedom that visitors to Las Vegas feel when partying there, the feeling that they could be whoever they wanted... and then go back to their normal everyday lives like nothing had happened. If nobody knows about the action, then it is not accountable, and no sin need be confessed.

I am not moralizing what is right or wrong, nor am I spewing condemnation, for I live in a glass house, and I am no angel. My children, when you get to be my age, sin is something you mostly remember. But no one escapes from where they have been. As long as we have memory, we recall our moves.

Indeed, glitter can bring a smile today. The Piper professes that a person can be instantly transformed by donning a wig, and stepping outside of one's self, that the answer to an imperfect situation lies elsewhere. That we deserve a fantastical evening incognito, unseen and unaffected by prying eyes.

Religions have explanations and answers for all this, predicated on the belief that God has given us free will, so we can be responsible for our decisions. But my point is that whatever happens in Vegas or Phoenix or Kathmandu... will stay with us for all of our days. The sly Vegas jingle is a lie.

A common thread running through Wavelengths is the joy of surfing the same wave as another soul, especially with a soulmate. When I have done *that*, my life has been complete.

THE STONE

"Look at that black and red stone," she says. "It is beautiful and must weigh 100 pounds."

"The stone is ugly," I reply. "It is not black and red, but brown and purple and must weigh 200 pounds."

How we perceive something does not change what it is.

The Old Testament says God created man in His own image. Since then, man has fashioned God in his own image. Some people perceive God as The Great Disciplinarian, while others see Him as the Very Definition of Love. Some say He carries a sword, while others say He carries us.

How we perceive God does not change who He is.

~~~~~~

Waited for the change
And while waiting I changed while
The stone stayed the same

~~~~~~

As I've grown grayer
Humbling years have bent my knees
Suitably for prayer

~~~~~~

IMMERSION

I believe Newbury nuts are tuned to the same Wavelength...

That would be Radio Heart and Soul on 112.1 MHz -

Just outside the FM dial.

MICKEY NEWBURY - CRYSTAL & STONE
New Introduction to the Second Edition

In 2004, the author published a biography on the legendary singer/songwriter, Mickey Newbury. A second edition was released in 2015. So that readers of Wavelengths *will understand who Newbury is, and the author's connection to him, that second preface in updated form follows below.*

In 1966 we lived in Maracaibo, where Dad operated an exploration-logging firm to service offshore drilling rigs. Tom Jones was popular then and there, and his "Funny Familiar Forgotten Feelings" dominated the radio airwaves. My Venezuelan buddies enjoyed "La Voz," and the structure of his hit seemed similar to the dramatic style of many Latin ballads. Our rock and roll band, Los Hippies, did not perform the song, reserving it for soft guitars and four-string cuatros at midnight beach parties on moonlit Lake Maracaibo.

March of 1968 found me in the United States Army at Fort Polk, Louisiana, mastering the mud-pit low-crawl. Guess you could say I had "Just Dropped In To See What Condition My Condition Was In." Though the rocker moved me, Black groups from my boot-camp unit congregated on barracks steps to harmonize Temptations material. That was fine with me, too. Great music.

Fast forward to 1974... University of California at Davis... a church social... my friend Jerry Freeman takes the stage. Jerry played great guitar, possessed a nice tenor voice and is one of the most gifted performers I have known. On that warm summer evening, he sang of *1912 in New York* and *Paris in the twenties* and *War is hell to live with*. In the midst of the trilogy, a simple chorus - repeated twice - hit me like a sledgehammer: *We're all building walls / They should be bridges.* Sometimes when I hear a great song, I have to remind myself to breathe. This was one of those times. As Jerry stepped from the stage, I stammered, "Wha... what in the world was that?" "A Mickey Newbury number," he replied. "Heaven Help The Child."

The following day found me in a record shop on a quest for Newbury music. Searching through alphabetical LPs, executing the drill Newbury fans know all too well: Willie Nelson... New Christy Minstrels... And there they were! Mickey Newbury records. I grabbed them all. Bought every Newbury album in the store. Paying quickly, I jumped on my old ten-speed and went home. Cueing up "Heaven," I sat back and closed my eyes. I have never recovered.

Something drew me to Newbury, an immediate, inexplicable connection. His musical style runs the gamut from country to folk to blues to bluegrass to easy listening to rock and roll. He mixes different genres in the same song, sometimes flavoring the tune with a dash of jazz or chamber music. Just as we use different tones of voice to communicate feelings, so he varies genus to match subject, often of epic or operatic proportion. His melodies carry simple words, easily remembered rhyme patterns with as many meanings as would be listeners. Riding the melody to deliver the lyric is that incredible voice, a haunting angelic tenor, boyishly young yet wise with wisdom.

On that California evening in 1974, I realized Newbury's ability to transcend musical genres made him great. But something else drew me to his music. He sounded familiar, plus the poetry made it clear he knew where I lived. As the bloke had written the soundtrack to my life, I was shocked and hooked.

A few Newbury releases materialized in record bins during the late seventies, and I snatched them up. His material disappeared for almost a decade, causing many fans to think he had departed the industry, perhaps the world. Then, in a new age - in the late eighties - I stumbled on his first compact disc. Pictured on the cover was an older Newbury, but glory hallelujah, the man was still here. After that, another hiatus until the mid-nineties.

Meanwhile, my wife Roxanne and I started a company to supply transmission systems to worldwide radio and television stations. We promptly hired a firm to set up our computer network. After the installation had been completed, a technician began teaching us how to navigate the web. "Anything you'd like to search for?" he asked. "Yes," I answered, and typed in "Mickey Newbury."

A few keystrokes and voilà, we were on Newbury's website. I could not believe that a cyber-gathering place existed with so many Newbury friends. In a few days, I was corresponding with him. In a few weeks, he telephoned. We talked many times for many hours and became friends. Though I tried, he would not let me hold him in awe. Then we met, and I caught his final public performance at the Songwriter's Festival in Gulf Shores, Florida.

Concurrently, I began to research Mickey Newbury, and that early study produced some good results. We continued to talk on the phone, for hours, about everything. We would see each other at a reunion in Oregon. A year later, I would visit him in his home. And then all too quickly, he was gone. But oh, the legacy.

Knowing Mickey and several of his friends inspired me to write this book, though caution flags appeared. His good friend, Larry Jon Wilson, wrote, "What Mickey Newbury was as a song crafter now belongs to the world of Chroniclers. I wish them a tiny fraction of his eloquence when they try to describe him." Larry Jon is absolutely right. Newbury is so loved... stripping away the myth... explaining the myth... is a mission littered with landmines.

Mickey was fragile and tough, like crystal and stone, transparent and rock-solid. The man was obliging and stubborn, open-minded and opinionated. He was a brilliant Bohemian and an unpretentious country boy. Loyal and fearless to a fault, he was a tender-hearted, spiritually perceptive Christian, a family man, a rambler at heart and perhaps bipolar. His wife Susan adds, "His life was a compilation of *Big Fish* and *O Brother, Where Art Thou?*" Mickey Newbury was Complex.

Distinguishing truth from fiction is the task. Personal agendas, individual bias and the aberration of time can shroud the subject in a Halloween costume. Every attempt has been made to unveil the subject. In some key instances, at least three sources were established to triangulate the truth. Interpolation - estimating a value that *lies* between known values - was cautiously employed. Perceived or contrived balance was not a goal, nor should it be.

Due to the complexity of the subject, others were recruited to speak here. More than 200 friends, peers and family members are quoted, and each person presents his or her truths about Newbury. In the end, oak, maple and pine become a forest, and we are left with a broader view.

This Herculean project was strengthened by conversations with Mickey, and his support is the book's foundation. There is a boundless depth to the man, a spirit that cannot be pinned down. These pages cannot contain that quintessence, but we can celebrate the art and life of this remarkable man, whose influence continues.

Crystal & Stone was published in 2004, and over the subsequent decade, I came across scores of new stories. By the time I began rewriting the book in 2014, some 500 pages of notes had been collected. Although my eyesight had worsened, I was able to see things in the dark that I could not see before. Or as my friend Roisin O'Rourke says, "Flashes from the lighthouse window."

Perhaps I had become more sensitive to subliminal wavelengths? Wherever the truth lies, the book was redone to integrate these bursts of illumination. Ultimately, 100 pages were added to the Second Edition in another attempt to chronicle the complex Mickey Newbury. The project could not have been completed without the love and patience of my wonderful wife Roxanne, and the assistance of Susan Newbury, Marty Hall, Craig Wilkins and RoRo.

Lastly, I wish to thank Mickey for his music and friendship and for enriching my composition, "I Remember When," with his **closing stanza:**

I remember when
We would chase the wind
And we caught it once or twice
I remember when

And I remember you
With your love so true
You never hurt me like I hurt you
I remember when

Oh then there came the day
When I sailed away
I said goodbye and then you prayed
I'd remember when

(chorus) But I remember when / We would chase the wind

You see I met a girl
Who means to me the world
We have pledged we will never say
I remember when

(chorus) But I remember when / We would chase the wind

Without the good
Without the bad
There would be no need my friend
To remember when

~*~

RON

I believe I was the first person from the Mickey Newbury web board to meet the well-known KCBS DJ, Ron Lyons. We began talking on the phone and exchanging e-mails during the winter of 1999. In early 2000, I visited Ron in his Bay Area home. While his wife Lana served up a tasty garlic chicken, Ron and I listened to Mickey's music and talked.

We had more than a few things in common, and we discussed children and broadcasting... but on this evening, Ron and I talked mainly about Mickey. We shared disappointment that he was not receiving his fair due. At the time, Mickey could not fight for himself. He was bedridden and slowly dying from a horrible disease that causes an irreversible scarring of the lungs.

Though it was terribly painful to do so, Mickey talked to us and sang for us. He always asked us how **we** were doing. We fell in love with the guy years after we had fallen in love with his music. Sometimes heroes disappoint. Mickey did not. We wanted to reciprocate.

Ron and I decided to get the word out about Mickey Newbury and his music. Ron would do something with audio, and I would write something and send it to anybody who would read it. I guess you could say we were two wild and crazy guys. Me and Ron against the world.

I cannot tell you how many artists and newspapers and radio stations were contacted. We were searching for an open door. Nobody seemed to care.

Meanwhile, I compiled a first list of Newbury songs recorded by other artists, and that initial effort was uploaded to the old songs.com website in early 2000. That research and probably 100 hours of intimate conversation with Mick paved the way for a second project. I wrote a 6,000-word article initially titled TCB and sent Ron several drafts, which he eagerly reviewed and critiqued. He encouraged me, and I did my best to help and encourage him.

When Ron's legendary friend - Ben Fong-Torres - told him that TCB would never get published, I was devastated. A few weeks later, after Rolling Stone turned it down ("It's not right for The Stone!"), the editorial was published by Goldmine magazine in June of 2000. The piece was the first significant article about Newbury to appear in a major publication in a decade.

Mickey was ten times happier for me (that my article had been published), than he was for himself (that significant publicity had been provided). If you knew Mickey, you will understand.

Around this time, Ron began working on an audio tribute. His initial effort produced a 45-minute CD, which never went to press. Ron had so much more to say about the man. We never tried to make Mick more than he was, but Mick was so much more than anybody we had met.

Ron and I would feed each other daily information and suggestions and hope, and this symbiotic relationship went on for more than three years. We were stubborn and focused and passionate, and though we had a few spirited discussions along the way, we always agreed about the objective of our work. We had a higher purpose, a calling, as we saw it.

Ron's wonderful two-CD tribute, *An American Treasure*, and the biography, Crystal & Stone, might not have happened without our dynamic friendship. Without Ron's intelligent cynicism (motivated me) and wry sense of humor (made me not take it so seriously), the book might not have come to pass. We spurred each other on when naysayers told us to turn around.

As we age, we have a romantic tendency to look back on fading landscapes. This one gives me goosebumps. I do not believe in destiny, as that train of thought is just too depressing. My sincere belief is that God gives us free will, and we are responsible for our choices.

But there was something else going on.

~~~~~~

A DAY WITH THE MICK

Gratefully accepting the invitation, I boarded an airplane and flew to Oregon. Mickey was sick, and I wanted to spend time with him before it was too late. Though I did not know what to expect, it was an eye-opening experience to visit Mickey in his Springfield home on May 16, 2001.

As I arrived at the farmhouse, Steve let me know I was at the right place. "Dad is inside," he quickly confirmed. Stepping into the modest residence, I found Mickey's room and stood in the doorway. If you had the experience of greeting Mickey Newbury, you know what comes next. His eyes twinkled. His sly smile sparkled. His focus made you feel like you were the Only One.

Alas, only a few people realize how terribly ill he was during his final days. A chain-smoker of filterless Camels for 40 years, Mickey had developed pulmonary fibrosis, a nasty disease similar to emphysema. The illness had weakened him to the point where he was almost completely bedridden. Chained to a hissing oxygen machine and bounded by four bedroom walls, he relied on telephone and computer for connection to the outside world.

Refusing to broadcast his demise for empathy, sympathy or monetary gain, he would instead express concern for others. Sidestepping his grave state, he demanded reports on my children and mutual friends.

And so, while lying in bed (Mickey would like that line), we had a day to discuss kids, friends, Texas, music, movies, politics, how prayer works, past lives, computers (Bill Gates is to blame), Leonardo da Vinci's paintings, the Old Testament, the relation of Genesis to Darwin's Theory of Evolution... and Newbury's inventions, such as a device that keeps a guitar in tune.

For his 61st birthday on May 19, I had taken him a 1000-page picture book, titled Millennium In Pictures. Casually thumbing through the weighty volume, Mick explained dozens of pictures in great detail without reading captions. For example, we both recognized the picture of the Empire State Building, while Mick proclaimed, "102 floors and over 6,000 windows..."

Though we discussed many things, he would always go several levels deep. He was well versed on the topic of human evolution, considering it was against the law to teach it in the Houston schools he attended in the fifties. Newbury also outlined his detailed theory on the origin of different races.

From there we went to the <u>Bible</u>, which was on his night stand. Turning to Genesis 1:26, Mick read, "Then God said, Let Us make man in Our image, according to Our likeness..." Mick said that "Us and Our" is proof there is more than one God. "The Trinity," I submitted. "Yes, a plurality," he replied. A few days after my visit, Mick sent me a note: "That leaves me with the conclusion that there must be more than one God. I choose to follow Jesus for I believe he was God come to earth to understand me. That could not have been one of his most pleasant decisions."

And then, we discussed painting. "Let me tell you a story about Leonardo da Vinci's *Last Supper*. He had painted the tablecloth with immaculate picture-in-picture detail. When da Vinci asked his students what they noticed about the exquisite painting, they replied, 'Why master, the beautiful tablecloth!' That same day da Vinci painted over the tablecloth with a brilliant white, because he wanted Jesus to be the focus of the painting. That teaches us," Mick summarized, "a great deal about not just painting, but life."

"I wanted to be a painter," he continued. "Had an art scholarship, but now I would just stare at a blank canvas for hours." Next, Mickey taught me how to draw. He turned a simple cartoon illustration upside down, and I drew it. Mick explained the technique works as the mind focuses on one line at a time.

All this talking must have made him thirsty, as he turned to me and asked, "Say Joe, do you know how to make coffee?" After answering affirmatively, I found myself in the kitchen trying to figure out how java was prepared in the Newbury household. Not finding a coffee pot, I recruited son Chris for instructions. We boiled water in a sauce pan and poured the water through a strainer. It should be mentioned that Newbury's preferred blend, a strong Indonesian Sumatra, could fuel a nuclear reactor. As I gave the cup to Mick, he thanked me and quipped, "Joe with a cuppa joe."

Mickey needed a little assistance with his computer, an Apple laptop running OS 6.1 and Netscape 4.5. In a simple spreadsheet, he had entered names, phone numbers and email addresses of many people, perhaps 100 in total. The list served as a key tool for Mickey to be able to reach out to friends. Problem was, the list was not in any kind of order, and when Mick wanted to find someone, he had to search the entire contact list. "I wish this mess was in some kind of order," he exclaimed. Without thinking, I reached over and clicked on the "Name" field, and presto... all the names were alphabetized. "Joe, you're a smart dude," said Mickey in his deep, gravelly voice.

Lost for words, feeling more like a smart ass that I had embarrassed Mickey, I said something like, "happy to help." He picked up on this immediately. "Joe," he said, "you have no idea how much this helps me. I was spending hours looking for people!" And then, he showed me how he amused himself by chasing spiders around the room with a laser pointer.

After terrorizing a few spiders, he demonstrated how energy flows between people. At a distance of one foot, Mickey asked me to look him in the eyes. He gazed at me with one eye for a few seconds and then both eyes at once. When he turned full vision on me... Pow! The energy flow was immediate. Mickey explained his belief that most people are on different frequencies, and one's frequency is transmitted by this energy. We can be on the same wavelength as another person, and this serves as an explanation of soulmate.

Mickey said this is how prayer works, how Jesus hears everyone, sort of like a spiritual, wideband radio transceiver. The proposition that thought travels, that thought can be transmitted and received, is not a novel concept. But the narrative illustrates how Newbury dug deeper into established hypotheses.

In the same spirit, vis-à-vis Newbury's deep songwriting, he described himself as "just a conduit." "Good writers," he said, "can't take credit for their work. All they can do is take credit for workin' hard for people who receive it." Novelist Ray Bradbury expressed the same thought: "I'm not in control of my muse. My muse does all the work." Like Bradbury and a short list of artists, Mick's perceived sentience to directional wavelengths explains his remarks. He believed in spiritual connection and knowingly made the point clear to me.

We were a few hours into the visit before the discussion turned to music. Interesting to note, the remastered CD of George Harrison's *All Things Must Pass* was laying on the bed. Mick was a fan of the Beatles, especially the album, *Revolver*. "Lennon and McCartney were perfectly matched," he said. "They needed each other like Bernie Taupin and Elton John."

We talked about Mick's album covers. He explained that the cover of *Lulled By The Moonlight*, which shows a feminine lady with flowing, auburn hair, was from an 1890 glass photo. "It was difficult to obtain the reproduction. The old glass image shattered immediately after we obtained a master copy. That's the exact cover I had in mind."

"Mick, that cover reminds me of the lady in the movie, *Somewhere In Time*."
"One of my favorite movies, Joe. I like movies where they build the story around the music, instead of the other way around. The Italians do this well. I love *The Graduate* for the same reason."

Mickey wanted me to know (said, "I want you to know...") "My music is the best part of me, but music is a partial picture of who I am. My music presents my best and most beautiful side, but it is not a complete representation." Mickey told me he had many dark sides and that he should take medication, but he refused, as it would stifle his creativity. "I lose myself in my music," he continued. "It's like I'm flying. I feel my music hypnotizes, and I'm a good hypnotist. I feel closest to my nature when I am writing songs. I don't like rap music because it does not have a melody." Then, he sang a parody-rap version of his sixties tune, "T. Total Tommy."

Out of the blue, Mick proposed an idea, which demonstrates his proactive concern for friends. Knowing my background in the radio broadcast industry, he said, "You should start a radio program, *Never Trust Anyone Under 40*." Buy radio time in a city like San Francisco, and hire Ron Lyons to do the programming. Trade-name this program title. Play music from the forties, fifties and sixties. This major sector (the baby boomers) has lots of money. It would be a huge success."

About this time, Laura Shayne brought home a stray dog, a big brown one. While she did her begging best to persuade Dad to let her keep the animal, he jokingly said, "Seems I've been takin' care of kids and dogs all my life." After resolving the canine question ("No!"), Mick attempted to play the piano and sing a new song. He was unable to do so, as he needed to return to bed for a breathing treatment.

"Say, Joe, do you know anything about oxygen," Mick asked as I wondered why I had studied psychology instead of medicine. "No," I answered. "Why?" "Well, could you make sure the output of the concentrator machine is on 2?" As my heart rate increased, I followed the tubing outside the room to the machine. After carefully cleaning my reading glasses, I set the dial to 2.000. Double and triple checked.

While we had been in the studio, I had noticed an old cardboard box in the corner containing several sheets of yellow, legal-size paper with handwriting. Mick told me the pages held the hand-written lyrics to many of his songs.

After I insisted that they should be framed and displayed on a museum wall, he shrugged and told me to choose one. He gave me the original handwritten lyrics to "East Kentucky," which he had penned in the early seventies.

When I returned to the bedroom with my treasure, Mickey looked me in the eyes while he grimly said, "I would like to be around to see my kids grow up. But Newbury men don't live very long. We're like comets. We burn brightly, but not for long. Right now, I'm a few years past my scheduled time to depart this planet, so my health is not an issue. My mind thinks in 3:4 time."

Mickey's words took me to his song, "The Future's Not What It Used To Be," to prophetically, self-fulfilling verses - which he had written 30 years earlier:

> I never thought I would live to grow old
> Oh the past cut a whole deep in me
> But there was a chance
> To be here a while longer
> At least I wanted to be

We heard footsteps in the hallway, and Mickey smiled as his lovely wife, Susan, stepped into the room. She was just home from her job as a school teacher. "Good news," Susan said, as she held up a letter. "You have been approved for medical assistance." They celebrated for a few minutes, and I sensed that my ailing friend was tired, and it was time for me to go.

Though Mickey protested, he absolutely needed to rest. We hugged and for the second time that day, I was not sure what to say. And so, I simply said, "Love ya, pal." The last words I heard before departing? "Love ya too, Joe." My head was spinning as I left the Newbury farm. We had covered so much ground and sky... seemed as if I had been there for a month. But actually, the time had flown.

I was fortunate to have received another invitation, to spend the night in the home of my good friend, Marty Hall. He lived close to the Newbury's, and he had experienced The Mick many times. Before I spoke a word, Marty knew.

When I returned home, Mickey wrote to me, "It is rough, this ole life, and I suppose it was supposed to be, for how else could we appreciate what is to come. A man who cannot see is never blinded by the lights, but he also lives his life in the darkness. This world is as close to hell as we'll get. We do get a taste of heaven here now and then."

MAGGIE THE BOHEMIAN

1973 was a good year for 33-year-old singer-songwriter Mickey Newbury. Competing in Tokyo with artists from 36 countries, he won the World Song Contest, performing his "Heaven Help the Child." A multilevel odyssey woven from threads of life as seen through his eyes, the ballad speaks of *1912 in New York* and *Paris in the 20's*, then rolls into *War is hell to live with...* concluding with the bittersweet farewell to the old year, "Auld Lang Syne." Between "Paris" and "War," Newbury delivers a transcendental passage: *We're all building walls / They should be bridges.*

The verse feels biblical, akin to <u>New Testament</u> verse. By no means is the author comparing Newbury's writing to the word of God. But this writer is saying unequivocally... Mickey Newbury was deeply influenced by The Word. "Heaven's" melody, complete with the ringing of church bells, is gorgeous, and Newbury's singing is stunning... as the song begins:

1912 in New York I take a walk up to Park Avenue
To sip some brew with my good friend
Maggie the Bohemian she was quite a woman of the world
I was the envy of the men
Heaven help the child heaven help the child

Paris in the '20's why it can offer plenty
to a young man with a vision so they say
With a friend named Fitzgerald I am headed for the old world
on a merchant steamer bound for Biscay Bay
Heaven help the child heaven help the child
Take him back to where he's never been

We're all building walls they should be bridges
We're all building walls they should be bridges

Nothin' like a freight train get you to the city
Would you pick another sad song for me Jim
I hate to leave the old man all alone to work the cotton
But the country never seems to bother him

Heaven help the child heaven help the child
Heaven help the children find their way

War is hell to live with I said to the general
as we made the battle plans out for the day
This will be the last one only God be willing
We can go back home this time to stay

If old acquaintance be forgotten and never brought to mind
Let's sip a cup of kindness then my friends to days gone by

Like most Newbury songs, "Heaven" is constructed with open architecture. While fans are free to draw their own interpretations from his deep poetry, just like Newbury's "33rd of August," lyrics in "Heaven" can point to the Bible. Consider the following:

1912 in New York

In Matthew 19:12 of the New Testament, Jesus states a saintly reason not to marry: "There are eunuchs who have made themselves eunuchs for the kingdom of heaven's sake." This apostolic teaching explains why celibacy is an answer for some of God's followers. And perhaps the Lord was telling the apostles why He did not marry Mary Magdalene.

I take a walk up to Park Avenue

After the Last Supper, which was eaten in the Upper Room on Mount Zion, Jesus walked up to the Garden of Gethsemane, a beautiful park where olive trees from His time are still growing strong. In the Bible, travelling "up" means going to a place of spiritual ascent, such as going up to Jerusalem.

To sip some brew with my good friend

At the Last Supper, "When He (Jesus) had taken a cup and given thanks, He gave it to them (the apostles, all Jews), and they all drank from it." (Matthew 26:27) Note also that the word "Brew" is slang for Hebrew or Jew. In the next three words of the song, Newbury states who is the "good friend" with whom the Star of the story sips some brew:

Maggie the Bohemian Lord she was quite a woman of the world

Maggie is a nickname for Magdalene, and Mary Magdalene is mentioned a dozen times in the Gospels. She was a Bohemian in her wanderings and, at the time, unconventional beliefs. Not only was she a strong, well-to-do woman who lived her beliefs in a patriarchal world, but she also was a visionary with the ability to understand new concepts. The proof? After He rose from the dead, Jesus first appeared to Mary Magdalene. (John 20:16)

I was the envy of the men

One of the strangest lyrics in a Newbury song is *I was the envy of the men*. This is unusual verbiage from Newbury because he did not speak that way. As he was a humble guy, "envy" must point to someone else. Combing the Bible for an instance of "envy," a passage jumps out: "Pilate answered them, saying, 'Do you want me to release for you the King of the Jews?' For he was aware that the chief priests had handed Him over because of **envy**." (Mark 15:9-10) Also, Mary Magdalene might have been *the envy of the men*.

Heaven help the child heaven help the child

When Baby Jesus was born, prophesies of the Old Testament were fulfilled, benefiting heaven and earth. (Isaiah 7:14, Micah 5:2, Jeremiah 23:5) Heaven helped the Child, and the Child heaven helped. Newbury explained to the author that his poetry is sometimes best understood by beginning the read from an *alternate* point on the line.

Paris in the '20's why it can offer plenty

After the crucifixion of Jesus, it is generally believed that Mary Magdalene escaped by boat to France, to the shores of Provence, south of Paris... where the Bohemian movement of free spirits would land 20 centuries later.

To a young man with a vision so they say

As a foretold end-times event, *they* (the prophets Joel and Saint Peter) say: "And it shall come to pass in the last days, says God, That I will pour out of My Spirit on all flesh; Your sons and your daughters shall prophesy; Your young men shall see visions." (Acts 2:17)

With a friend named Fitzgerald I am headed for the old world

Old world refers to ancient times and tradition of the eastern hemisphere, figuratively... salvation. *Fitzgerald* refers to novelist F. Scott Fitzgerald, who along with Ernest Hemingway, led the Bohemian movement in Paris (western hemisphere / lost generation) in the 1920's, figuratively... sin.

From an article titled, *Searching for Paradise*, William Doino Jr. writes: "Despite his personal life, Fitzgerald never let go of his religious foundations. He had a conscience and tried to make amends to those he had wronged, even as he kept slipping back into sin. Biblical references and images appear in his writings, especially during his most severe trials." This was Newbury's wavelength; in the old world, Fitzgerald and Newbury would seek the New Jerusalem.

On a merchant steamer bound for Biscay Bay

Though Mary Magdalene would have landed on the southeast side of France in ~45 AD, there is a Bay of Biscay on the southwest side of France. And as for sharing a ride with Fitzgerald on the sea vessel... in 1945, the New England Shipbuilding Corp. christened a new member to the Liberty Ship family, the "SS F. Scott Fitzgerald," a 422-foot merchant steamer.

Heaven help the child heaven help the child
Take him back to where he's never been

As written by Apostle John: (in heaven) "God will wipe away every tear from their eyes; there shall be no more death, nor sorrow, nor crying. There shall be no more pain, for the former things have passed away." (Revelation 21:4)

We're all building walls they should be bridges
We're all building walls they should be bridges

These lyrics feel like New Testament teaching... as Paul the Apostle says, "For He Himself is our peace, who has made both one, and has broken down the middle wall of separation." (Ephesians 2:14) Also, Isaiah 59:2 teaches that "your iniquities (sins) have separated you from your God..." Christians believe the only bridge from earth to heaven is through Jesus.

Nothin' like a freight train get you to the city
Would you pick another sad song for me Jim

Newbury had a longing for a better place, and train was a means to an end. "Jim" is a nickname for James, the brother of Jesus, AKA "James the Less." The first bishop of Jerusalem, James sang at the first ever mass there. Down to a more obvious meaning, "Jim" is a shout out to Jimmie Rodgers, who worked on the railway and is regarded as the Father of Country Music. Rodgers was the preferred singer of Mickey's dad... saluted in the next line.

I hate to leave the old man <u>all alone to work the cotton</u>
But the country never seems to bother him

There are two specific meanings to these lines, one worldly, one divine:
1. In the 30's, Newbury's dad spent a few years in prison, a Texas hellhole, immortalized on Newbury's first single recording, "Eastham Prison Farm":
Pickin' that cotton, white cotton all day long
Puttin' that cotton in a seven-foot sack
Got a twelve-gauge shotgun at my back
Spendin' time on the Eastham Prison Farm

2. Upping the ante to a spiritual story from the <u>New Testament</u>, *I hate to leave the old man all alone to work the cotton* takes us to Matthew 4:21-22: "Going on from there, He (Jesus) saw two other brothers, James the son of Zebedee ("James the Great"), and John his brother, in the boat with Zebedee their father, *mending their nets*. He (Jesus) called them, and immediately they left the boat and their father, and followed Him."

Heaven help the child heaven help the child
Heaven help the children find their way

God surely wants the children to find their way, as stated in Mark 10:13-16: "Then they brought little children to Him, that He might touch them; but the disciples rebuked those who brought them. But when Jesus saw it, He was greatly displeased and said to them, 'Let the little children come to Me, and do not forbid them; for of such is the kingdom of God. Assuredly, I say to you, whoever does not receive the kingdom of God as a little child will by no means enter it.' And He took them up in His arms, laid His hands on them, and blessed them."

War is hell to live with I said to the general
As we made the battle plans out for the day
This will be the last one only God be willing

Jesus explained the final battle (*the last one only God be willing*) to His apostles: "And you will hear of wars and rumors of wars. See that you are not troubled; for all *these things* must come to pass, but the end is not yet. For nation will rise against nation, and kingdom against kingdom..." (Matthew 24:6-7)

We will go back home this time to stay

As for Newbury's prayer-verse... *we will go back home this time to stay...* the Bible says: "For the Lord Himself will descend from heaven with a shout, with the voice of an archangel, and with the trumpet of God. And the dead in Christ will rise first. Then we who are alive and remain shall be caught up together with them in the clouds to meet the Lord in the air. And thus we shall always be with the Lord." (1 Thessalonians 4:16-17)

If old acquaintance be forgotten and never brought to mind
Let's sip a cup of kindness then my friends to days gone by

With the closing lines borrowed from Scottish poet Robert Burns, the song circles back to the beginning, again to *sip some brew with my good friend.* Newbury completes "Heaven Help The Child" in ceremonial tradition, as in Luke 22:19 at the conclusion of the Last Supper, Jesus tells His chosen followers, "Do this in remembrance of Me."

Though Newbury was a student of the Bible, the above verses may not have been specifically at hand, in mind, when he wrote "Heaven Help The Child." However, the Bible and the teachings of Jesus were his solid foundation. Make no mistake about it, the man was a Christian, and he knew his faith.

Undeniably, "Heaven Help The Child" is a trilogy about times and places... 1912 in New York and Paris in the 20's and World War II. Third and fourth dimension stuff. The poetic lyrics can also be interpreted on a spiritual level. Regardless of interpretation, Newbury's song is a powerful demonstration of the richness of art derived from its many inspirations.

A WAVELENGTH THING

Like all great truths, the music of Mickey Sims Newbury is deceptively simple. On the wings of beautiful melody, his poetry soars straight into the hearts of souls receptive to the wavelength. This simple truth is why so many artists and well-tuned "passionates" are dumbstruck by the majesty of his art.

Artists are among the most highly tuned emotional souls on the blue marble, with an ability to home in on honest art. Many of these sensitive spirits "hear" what Newbury is really expressing and take his music to heart. The proof? 1,250 artists from 32 countries have drawn from the Newbury well to offer up almost 1,600 renditions of his songs.

It is difficult to make the following statement without sounding pretentious, but so be it: Only the very tiptop of the emotional food chain can hear him, and this explains why many creative artists have lined up to perform his music. This also explains why Mr. Newbury will never be popular with the masses. Not directly anyway.

Many people hear an echo of Newbury's music through their favorite outlet, and this reflection is from artists who have rendered the piper's tunes in 50 different genres of music... as pop, folk, funk, jazz, rock, soul, blues, R&B, country, bluegrass and easy listening. Also delivering Newbury's oeuvre are classical composers who speak gospel, opera, pipe organ and church choir. Several dancers have been moved too, interpreting the message as waltz, disco, polka, rumba, tango and reggae. And hard rockers have offered their take on Mick's music to followers of rap, punk, lo-fi, metal and psychedelia.

Endorsement by such a large, disparate group is more than just noteworthy. It is extraordinary. Speaking to old hippies and young yuppies, to the political left and right, to generation x, y and z... these artists speak to just about everybody. From a list of artists as diverse as Joan Baez and Perry Como, they communicate with the masses in the universal language.

Newbury said he was a songwriter first. He wrote with emotional sincerity for the emotionally sincere, and they hear him. It is a wavelength thing.

The comprehensive, 56-page list of songs written by Mickey Newbury, which have been covered by other artists, can be viewed at MickeyNewbury.com.

EXPLORACIÓN

Una inmersión profunda en Venezuela en español

El "Faro de Maracaibo" sobre el puente General Rafael Urdaneta de 5,4 millas

EL CIELO EN LA TIERRA:
LA VENEZUELA QUE FUE

Traducido por Augusto Socarrás

Como personajes de la vida real sacados de una novela de John Steinbeck, mis padres se fueron de Oklahoma después de la Segunda Guerra Mundial. Con todas sus posesiones atadas a la parte superior de un Plymouth de 1938, Kelly y LaWanda se unieron a la ola de emigración de la tierra pobre a la Tierra Prometida.

Junto con miles de "Okies", viajaron 1,800 millas en la Ruta 66, buscando trabajo, dignidad y un futuro. Fueron hacia el oeste por la Carretera Madre, todo el camino hasta el final de la línea, a la Tierra Dorada de California.

Nací en 1948 y pasé mis años de niñez en Bakersfield, una ciudad soleada, un rico pueblo petrolero y agrícola, poblado de soñadores y rufianes donde pelear era una forma aceptada de hacer amigos. Aunque la temperatura de la zona era caliente como el infierno, tengo buenos recuerdos de montar el río Kern, mucho antes de que el rafting se convirtiera en un deporte.

Cuando cumplí 12 años, papá se mudó con la familia al sur... a un área aún más calurosa en los tórridos trópicos... a un pueblo petrolero aún más rico... a Maracaibo, Venezuela, tierra mágica de perezosos, delfines de río, cocodrilos del Orinoco y osos hormigueros gigantes. Una tierra donde mi hermana y yo nos sentimos como los únicos rubios del país.

Venezuela es productor de petróleo desde hace 100 años, y con 300 mil millones de barriles tiene el alijo de petróleo más grande de cualquier nación. Papá fue allí en 1961 con la esperanza de ganar su fortuna como trabajador de plataformas para la Standard Oil de California (Chevron). Desde la perforación en alta mar en un lago poderoso hasta los rigores de los matorrales de Boscán, el trabajo era agotador y peligroso. Con cinco días de trabajo y cinco días de descanso, los perforadores necesitaban mantener un ojo en una grúa puente y otro ojo para criaturas coloridas y espeluznantes.

En verdad, la nación sudamericana ha sido bendecida con paisajes deslumbrantes. En su tercer viaje a las Américas en 1497, Colón navegó hasta la desembocadura del río Orinoco de Venezuela y declaró que había encontrado el "Cielo en la Tierra".

Apodada "Pequeña Venecia" por exploradores españoles - después de observar casas sobre pilotes sobre el agua - Venezuela es en verdad una tierra paradisíaca. Su diversa belleza se extiende desde los magníficos picos de las montañas de los Andes de 15,000 pies (en el oeste) ... a la selva amazónica de otro mundo (sur)... a 1,700 millas de majestuosa costa caribeña (norte)... hasta el caudaloso río Orinoco (este).

Aunque Venezuela se encuentra hoy en una situación desesperada debido a la corrupción de tiranos egoístas, fue una potencia económica vivaz en los años sesenta y setenta, cuando todas las piezas esenciales se juntaron. Al abandonar el gobierno autoritario en 1961, su constitución se inspiró en la constitución de los Estados Unidos. A continuación, la moneda, el bolívar, se fijó al dólar estadounidense a un tipo de cambio de 4,3 a 1.

Agregue un gobierno estable, producción masiva de petróleo más oro y diamantes...y el país estaba en camino alegre hacia la era más próspera de su historia. Una señal reveladora: sin duda, Venezuela tenía la clase media más grande de todos de América Latina. El consumo de whisky escocés fue el más alto del mundo; la clase media conducía Ford y Volkswagen y se iba de compras y juergas a Miami, donde eran conocidos como "dame dos."

Así llegamos al verano de 1961 justo cuando empezaba todo este cambio. Papá había organizado nuestro vuelo de 22 horas a Maracaibo a través del turbohélice de Pan Am. Ruta: Los Ángeles a México a Guatemala a Panamá a Colombia a Venezuela. En algún lugar sobre Colombia, chocamos con una turbulencia repentina y mortal, lo que provocó al avión entrar en picada pronunciada y girar lentamente. Todo el mundo estaba gritando, excepto mamá, que dijo: "¡Joe, aprieta el cinturón de seguridad de Paulette!"

Después de lo que pareció una eternidad, el piloto levantó el morro y nos recuperamos. Mamá se rió a carcajadas de que el hombre sentado detrás de nosotros había vomitado por todas partes sobre nuestra nueva ropa de viaje. Cuando aterrizamos, los médicos abordaron la nave y sacaron al piloto principal en una camilla. Se había lastimado la espalda al maniobrar el avión. ¿Qué aprendimos en este día? Primero, en un avión cayendo, no hay ateos. Y segundo, no hay nada mal con besar el suelo.

Después de besar el asfalto, lo primero que noté fue el calor. Me golpeó como un tren. Ubicado 10 grados al norte del ecuador y 70 millas al sur del Caribe,

Maracaibo es CALIENTE. Llegamos a junio con 95 grados de temperatura y 70% de humedad, que "se siente como" 124 grados.

En área de la aduana, entramos en una cola lenta que conducía a hombres uniformados, detrás de largas mesas. Cuando llegó nuestro turno unas tres horas más tarde, el que más enojado se veía comenzó nuestra inspección preguntando: "Tiene algo que desee declarar?" "No ahora", respondí en mi mejor personificación de "Honest Abe" (Abraham Lincoln). Mamá se mordió el labio cuando el molesto agente comenzó a hurgar en nuestras maletas. En retrospectiva, probablemente no estaba enojado el señor, solo caliente. Y ciertamente no estaba impresionado con un Gringo sabelotodo de 12 años. Un rostro pálido que medía 4'11".

Cuando salimos de la aduana, papá estaba allí esperándonos y rápidamente nos metió en un auto con el lujo indiscutible de los trópicos del tercer mundo... aire acondicionado. Durante los 30 minutos en coche hasta nuestro apartamento, me di cuenta de que todo el mundo en esta ciudad era venezolano... un pensamiento que era a la vez fascinante y aterrador. Y todos hablaban español. Estaba, por primera vez, en minoría.

Aún así, hay algo bastante mágico en comenzar de nuevo en otro país, es decir, ser sacado de la zona de confort de uno y llevado a un lugar con entorno totalmente diferente. No simplemente el paso de una página a un nuevo capítulo, sino una historia completamente nueva. Con nuevos amigos. Nuevos alimentos. Y un nuevo idioma.

Estábamos tan felices de estar en nuestro nuevo apartamento. Ubicado en Calle 67 entre Avenidas 3D y 3E, el edificio de tres pisos, Edificio Don Carlos, se asomaba sobre el pintoresco lago de Maracaibo, el lago más grande de toda América del Sur. Con 28 millones de años y alimentado por más de 135 ríos, es el tercer lago más antiguo del mundo. También es el área más activa para la caída de rayos en el planeta. Comúnmente llamado rayo del Catatumbo, durante las grandes tormentas, el "Faro de Maracaibo" produce frecuentemente más de 40 rayos por minuto. Desde el balcón de nuestro apartamento, a menudo disfrutábamos del asombroso espectáculo de luces de Dios. Una explosión de toda la noche de luz blanca irregular de los cielos.

En nuestra primera mañana en el apartamento, pensé que mamá estaba jugando a las charadas con la criada nueva, Selena. (Todo el mundo en Venezuela tiene sirvienta.) Con movimientos salvajes de su mano...

mamá estaba haciendo todo lo posible para "pedirle" que preparara avena para el desayuno. Mi hermana Paulette y yo vimos a Selena asentir cuando comenzó a hervir agua. Algunos minutos después, nos sirvió un tazón de caldo caliente. Selena había cocinado la avena, la coló y nos sirvió el jugo. "Gracias", le dijo mamá a Selena. "Bébetelo", dijo mamá a sus hijos.

Después del desayuno, bajé las escaleras hacia el exterior de nuestro apartamento. Allí vi a un niño un poco mayor que yo, que parecía ser venezolano. Ambos nos saludamos y le pregunté si le gustaría jugar un poco de "football". Sí, respondió, y ambos subimos corriendo a nuestros apartamentos. El regresó con una pelota redonda, negra y blanca, y regresé con una pelota de "football" americano. Una de mis primeras lecciones: la palabra para soccer en español es "fútbol."

El chico que conocí en junio de 1961 ha sido mi mejor amigo hasta el día de hoy. Augusto Socarras en realidad es colombiano y su familia vivía en el tercer piso de nuestro edificio, mientras vivíamos un piso más abajo. Tenía dos hermanos menores... Chemi de seis años y Cuchi - de cuatro... más tres hermanas menores, Carolina - de nueve, Clemencia - ocho y Elizabeth - uno. El papá de Augusto, Luis Napoleón Ferreira ("Napo"), fue un arquitecto brillante; y su madre, Ligia, se convirtió en segunda madre para mí. Casi al instante.

A veces en la vida, en los lugares más inesperados y bajo el escenario más extraño de las circunstancias, nos encontramos con alguien que está sintonizado con nuestra longitud de onda exacta. La ocasión es una rareza y una bendición. Augusto me tomó bajo su protección, y él me mostró las cuerdas. Yo era un extraño en suelo extranjero, y él hizo que me sintiera bienvenido. En mi primer día en otra tierra, no me sentí solo.

Una de las primeras cosas que me enseñó Augusto fue cómo decir las malas palabras en español. Siguen siendo una preferencia constante sobre sus homólogos ingleses. Maldecir en español suena mucho más romántico, además de enfático. Un adoctrinamiento a la lengua vernácula venezolana no sería completo, sin embargo, sin algunas palabras clave adicionales. Una persona de Maracaibo es un maracucho, y cuando quiere decir fantástico o genial, simplemente dice "chévere". Y si a un maracucho le preguntan cómo está, puede que responda, "machete", que significa estupendo.

Antes de que nos fuéramos de California, había estudiado español en el grado 7, y ese año de instrucción ayudó un poco. Pero mi hermana Paulette se convirtió en compañera de juegos con los hermanos y hermanas de Augusto, principalmente Cuchi, que tenía su misma edad. A los cuatro años estaba completamente inmersa en el idioma español, de una manera divertida, y dentro de unos seis meses, lo hablaba con fluidez. En corto plazo, Paulette se convirtió en la diplomática de la familia, especialmente cuando queríamos avena.

Nuestra familia estaba sumergida en la cultura latina y me encantaba. Si las pinturas de Norman Rockwell presentan la idílica familia sobre lienzo, luego la familia de Augusto, los Ferreira, podrían haber sido los modelos. Quiero decir, su familia era tan amorosa. Y respetuosa. Y humilde. Y sólida como una roca.

Encarnaron lo mejor de la cultura latina y los valores familiares. Sus prioridades eran Dios, la familia, el trabajo y el juego, en ese orden. "Todos para uno y uno para todos" era su lema tácito, y mantuvieron ese estándar todos los días. Después de ser "adoptado" por los Ferreira, mi sesgo Ugly American se niveló.

Una vez que mi cabeza estaba en orden, me divertí mucho durante mi primer año en Venezuela. Trepando cocoteros de 40 pies. Disfrutando de la playa virgen de La Cañada... un pueblo tranquilo cerca de Maracaibo, donde la gente y las olas rodaban lentamente. Atrapar iguanas verdes que crecen hasta cinco pies de largo y pesan 20 libras. Dormir en un colorido chinchorro... una hamaca tejida por los indios guajiros. Aprendiendo a rasguear el cuatro venezolano... un instrumento de cuatro cuerdas que suena como un encantador cruce entre una mandolina y una guitarra de 12 cuerdas.

Nadar en las aguas limpias y cristalinas de 87 grados del lago de Maracaibo, una experiencia regeneradora que me hizo "renacer". Y debemos incluir cocinar un cerdo entero en el suelo, al estilo hawaiano. Pocos gustos en este mundo se comparan con el primer bocado de cerdo que se acaba de caer de los huesos de un cerdo que estuvimos dos días asando y oliendo... lo que nos lleva a la cocina local. Influenciado por muchas culturas románticas europeas y tradiciones indígenas, la comida venezolana es deliciosa más allá de las palabras.

La discusión debe comenzar con las arepas, piedra angular de la dieta venezolana. Hechas de masa de maíz y de aproximadamente media pulgada de espesor, las arepas se fríen o se asan a la parrilla y típicamente se rellenan con mantequilla y queso blanco. Los ingredientes pueden incluir carne de res, pollo, cerdo, frijoles negros, aguacate y huevos. Puestos de arepa en la calle esquinas por todo Maracaibo, donde por sólo dos bolívares (unos 45 centavos de dólar), podrías comprar una deliciosa arepa rellena con lo que tu corazón deseara. Después de las fiestas de adolescentes nocturnas, Augusto y yo podíamos encontrarnos en nuestro amado puesto de arepas en la avenida Bella Vista.

En las fiestas de adolescentes, donde disfrutamos del giro de Chubby Checker en esta era, el anfitrión servía tequeños, una harina de trigo frita con queso blanco adentro. Un plato de ocho de ellos se vendía en la mayoría de los clubes y en las esquinas de las calles por un Bolívar. El anfitrión también puede servir empanadas, un refrigerio de harina de maíz que contiene queso blanco o carne deshebrada. En Navidad disfrutábamos de hallacas, una mezcla al vapor de carne de res, cerdo, pollo, alcaparras, pasas y aceitunas envueltas en harina de maíz y atado con una cuerda dentro de hojas de plátano. Y mientras camina en cualquier lugar, deliciosos mangos estaban a nuestra entera disposición. Nosotros solo alcanzar y arrancarlos de los árboles.

Si tuviéramos calor y sed, como suele ser el caso en Maracaibo, buscaríamos un burro o una carreta tirada por una bicicleta vendiendo cepillaos. El vendedor rasparía un gran bloque de hielo con un cepillo rígido para recoger "hielo de nieve" para llenar un vaso de plástico. Elegiríamos entre sabores naturales, como menta, coca, guayaba, mango, limón, plátano, coco y piña. Como gran final, el vendedor remataba el sabor con una leche condensada. ¿El precio de esta celestial mezcla? Un medio (25 centavos venezolanos) o un níquel americano.

Además de los cepillaos, había disponibles varios calmantes para la sed. En todas partes se vendían deliciosas bebidas de frutas naturales. Coca Cola tuvo su planta embotelladora en Maracaibo. Las cervezas elaboradas localmente incluían Zulia y Polar, ambas con 5% de alcohol. El ron oscuro venezolano fue particularmente popular, y Ron Añejo fue la marca preferida.

Era una mezcla suave de varios rones envejecidos por un período mínimo de dos años en barricas de roble blanco. Aunque yo probé la fruta prohibida, yo era realmente demasiado joven para participar.

Por sólo la mitad del precio de un cepillao (una locha), los vendedores ambulantes que llevan grandes los termos plateados vendían espressos mucho antes de la existencia de Starbucks. Procedente de granos cultivados localmente, el café fuerte se sirvió caliente, negro y súper dulce. Un estimulante en una taza Dixie, este satisfactorio trago único fue la última sacudida de energía.

Recuerdo un día que estaba arruinado y quería un espresso. Como la necesidad es la madre de la invención, ideé una estrategia efectiva para obtener un café gratis. Hablando con un amable vendedor ambulante, entré en mi primera negociación comercial.

"Hola, amigo", le dije al vendedor. "¿Cómo está tu café hoy?"
"Es bueno, señor".
"Sé que lo es. Como cliente leal, siempre trato de tomar mi café aquí".
"Gracias, señor", dijo el vendedor con aprecio.
"Pero hoy estoy triste porque no puedo comprar tu café".
"¿Por qué no, señor?"
"No puedo disfrutar de tu café porque hoy estoy sin dinero".
"Ay, señor, lo siento."
"Lo siento también, porque sé que quieres ver felices a tus clientes".
"Sí, señor, eso es correcto".
"Como cliente feliz, vengo aquí muchas veces porque me encanta su café".
"Gracias, señor", dijo el vendedor con aprecio.
"Y por supuesto, ¿sabes que volveré a disfrutar de tu café?"
"Sí, señor, eso espero", dijo el vendedor en tono más bajo.
"Pero hoy desearía ser feliz".
"Ay, señor, es sólo café", dijo el vendedor mientras miraba hacia otro lado.
"Sí, pero me levanta, y luego puedo seguir mi camino".
"Está bien, señor, le invitaré a un cafecito, y luego lo veré mañana".

El café que me sirvió ese día el amable vendedor fue una sacudida de satisfacción. Esta capacitación básica era importante porque la mayoría de los bienes en Venezuela eran negociables. Una excepción fue en las grandes tiendas, donde se fijaron los precios.

Maracaibo tuvo los primeros supermercados en Venezuela, una cadena llamada "Todos" que era propiedad de la destacada familia Rockefeller. La ciudad también contaba con una tienda por departamentos Sears, ubicada en la avenida 5 de Julio. Todos y Sears eran lugares de compras de moda para los lugareños, debido a la extensa selección de productos de calidad, precios competitivos y sí, aire acondicionado.

Pero la limpieza, la comodidad y el aire acondicionado no fueron rival para la emoción de las compras del casco antiguo. Había cigarros cubanos y pinturas al óleo originales. Monos mascotas y cadenas de oro de 18 kilates. Tocadiscos y zapatos de cocodrilo. El olor de las arepas y el café se mezclaba con los humos de los autobuses y el sudor de los animales.

Ubicado al pie de Maracaibo cerca de coloridas casas históricas coloniales, en el Maracaibo Viejo, está el centro original. Casi cualquier cosa podría negociarse allí, incluyendo, estoy seguro, contrabando, parejas de baile y pociones alucinantes. Aunque nuestra familia compraba frutas, verduras y pescado fresco en Centro, nunca sabíamos lo que podríamos ver, oír u oler. Había tiendas con frentes tradicionales y vendedores en la calle. Había corredores que podían encontrar cualquier cosa, vender lo que fuera. Señor, ¿le gustaría ver un loro azul y dorado?

Nuestra familia bajó muchas veces al casco antiguo para comprar, visitar la oficina de correos y tomar el ferry. En 1961, papá a menudo cruzaba en ferry el lago de Maracaibo hasta la pujante ciudad de Cabimas, centro de producción petrolera, o al campo petrolero Boscán. Para tomar el ferry ("la flecha") desde el antiguo muelle de Calle 100, teníamos que estar en la fila de carros a las 4:00 AM. Con suerte, estaríamos en camino a las 7:00 AM, justo antes de que el sol comenzara a cocinar la ciudad. Esperando en la fila, siempre estábamos entretenidos por el desfile interminable de vendedores ambulantes insistentes en nuestra ventana, vendiendo de todo, desde cinturones hasta balas y baterías.

En agosto de 1962, el transbordador siguió el camino del coche de caballos cuando se inauguró el puente General Rafael Urdaneta, que conecta a Maracaibo con Cabimas y el oriente venezolano. Esta maravilla de la construcción tardó cinco años en completarse, y con 5,4 millas de largo, tiene siete veces la longitud del puente Golden Gate.

No solo disfrutamos de una vista perfecta del puente desde el balcón de nuestro apartamento, sino que el nuevo puente le ahorró a papá 10 horas por semana. Para su bienestar físico, eso fue una gran cosa. El pobre llegaba a casa sucio y muerto de cansancio de trabajar en una torre caliente de perforación de petróleo en Boscán o en una plataforma de perforación en el medio del lago. Con un horario brutal de cinco días seguidos, el hombre necesitaba recuperarse. Pero Kelly Ziemer estaba orgulloso de ser un trabajador de Okie-Bakersfield, y sí, le gustaba la música de Merle Haggard. Ray Charles también.

Papá fue muy bien compensado por el arduo trabajo, y después de unos seis meses, nuestra familia había acumulado un poco de ahorro. Mis padres comenzaron a ahorrar dinero para comprar una casa, además de que podíamos permitirnos comer fuera... de vez en cuando.

La comida callejera en Maracaibo era deliciosa y los restaurantes eran sublimes. Mi restaurante favorito en el mundo estaba (y sigue estando) ubicado en la esquina de Avenida 3H y Calle 76. "Mi Vaquita" abrió sus puertas unos seis meses después de nuestra llegada al país. Pediríamos la parrillada mixta, y aunque el menú decía que serviría a dos personas, papá y yo ordenábamos la nuestra. El camarero desplegaría un pequeño asador al lado de la mesa. Chisporroteando en la parrilla había varios cortes selectos de carne sazonada, incluyendo chuletas de cordero, hígado de res, pechuga de pollo, chorizo y filetes de seis onzas. El jugoso bistec provenía de ganado 100% alimentado con pasto, y el dulce aroma de ese magnífico servicio vive en mi memoria hasta el día de hoy.

Otro restaurante popular frecuentado por los Ziemer estaba ubicado en la Avenida 23, entre Calles 66 y 67. Mucho menos costoso que el exaltado Mi Vaquita, el restaurante Rincón Boricua era uno de los favoritos de los niños. Con karts, juegos de carnaval y una gran pantalla al aire libre con dibujos animados y películas, Rincón servía el mejor pollo asado en canasta que he probado en mi vida. Acompañada de yuca y papas fritas, esta delicia de la cena estaba disponible por solo 8 Bs. Entonces, por $ 1.85 US, nos sentábamos afuera en mesas de picnic, en la noche cuando el sol caliente se había puesto y la noche era fresca, comiendo pollo crujiente y disfrutando de la última película de "Los tres chiflados".

Como el costo de la gasolina local era muy bajo, el transporte por la ciudad era ridículamente barato. Los buses públicos cuestan un medio (25 venezolanos centavos o solo un centavo americano), pero generalmente estaban llenos de gente. Si el espacio para estar de pie no era su preferencia, entonces había "carritos" disponibles; estos automóviles de pasajeros (Ford, Chevrolet, lo que sea) seguían una ruta específica. Una persona esperaría un carrito (como esperar un autobús), y el conductor lo llevaría a cualquier lugar a lo largo de la ruta designada. Perfectamente seguros y limpios, los carritos circulaban todo el día y la mayor parte de la noche. ¿El costo para ir a la mayoría de los lugares en carrito? Un real o 50 centavos venezolanos (12 centavos de dólar estadounidense).

Augusto y yo tomamos carritos todo el tiempo y nunca tuvimos ningún problema. Las calles de Maracaibo eran seguras y pacíficas, nunca una amenaza de peligro. Los maracuchos eran amigables, amantes de la diversión e independientemente de su posición en la vida, la mayoría de los lugareños harían todo lo posible para ayudar a una persona necesitada.

Una persona sola no caminaría por un callejón oscuro en Centro a las 3 AM, agitando billetes de 100 dólares en el aire. Pero el caso es que Augusto y yo nunca experimentamos una crisis, nunca nos sentimos vulnerable en las serenas calles de Maracaibo. Antes de que nos dirigiéramos a las luces brillantes, la madre de Augusto, Ligia, nos bendecía, diciendo "Dios los bendiga", mientras hacía la señal de la cruz en el aire. Su bendición me hizo sentir como si estuviera usando un escudo invisible. Sintiéndonos seguros y con gran expectativa de una velada divertida, Augusto y yo iríamos de fiesta el sábado con los otros muchachos, con sensatez, pero el domingo, por nuestra propia voluntad, a menudo íbamos a la iglesia.

¿Adónde iríamos en un carrito? A los clubes deportivos. Al cine. A visitar amigos. Pasábamos horas y horas en los clubes deportivos, nadando, comiendo tequeños y echando un vistazo a las hermosas chicas. "Chicas hermosas" no es solo una opinión. Venezuela se ha llevado ocho títulos de Miss Internacional, siete títulos de Miss Universo, seis títulos de Miss Mundo y dos títulos de Miss Tierra, por lo que es el único país en ganar los cuatro concursos varias veces. Las hermosas chicas venezolanas parecía que estaban en todas partes, especialmente en los clubes, y eran muy amables.

La mayoría de los clubes tenían piscinas olímpicas, canchas de tenis y comedores. El Club Creole y el Club Bella Vista fueron nuestros favoritos...

pero también disfrutamos de Club Alianza, Club Náutico, Club Comercio y por supuesto, el lujoso Hotel Del Lago. Los clubes organizaban fiestas los fines de semana, pero Augusto y yo no podíamos permitirnos ser miembros de todos los clubes de la ciudad. Y así, siempre encontramos alguna manera de ser invitados. ¿Qué hacíamos en estas fiestas? Bailábamos.

La música estaba viva. Como una especie de criatura mística, nos atraparía y les diría a nuestros pies qué hacer. El Flautista de Hamelín de la Danza, la gaita Zuliana, es una música bailable que se originó en Maracaibo en los años 60's. En su forma más primitiva, los cantantes van acompañados de instrumentos folclóricos básicos, como el tambor furro, cuatro, maracas, tambora y charrasca. Los músicos venezolanos infundieron la gaita tradicional con un chupito de salsa caliente y una medida dulce de merengue... agregando conga y trompeta y bajo... y movimientos de cadera exagerados fueron desatados. Venezolanos alegres moviéndose en la pista de baile repleta fueron una presencia supremamente confiada y serena en el ritmo eterno. Esta era, después de todo, su música. Su fiesta. Su celebración de la vida.

Tenían tanto que celebrar, para empezar, el compañerismo de la gente... Incluso con extraños, la amabilidad fue excepcional y algo que yo no había experimentado. También fueron bendecidos de vivir en uno de los más bellos entornos del planeta con espectaculares playas, montañas y selvas.

Además, como disfrutaban de los ingresos medios más altos de todos América Latina, su nivel de vida se había disparado a su nivel más alto jamás visto. En otras palabras, podían permitirse comprar buena comida, un automóvil, unas vacaciones. Finalmente, el gobierno estaba realizando importantes mejoras en la infraestructura mediante la construcción de nuevas escuelas, nuevos hospitales, nuevas carreteras y nuevos puentes. Cualquiera que fuera la dirección que uno miraba, la nación estaba haciendo cambios que alteraban la vida. Y así, la gente bailó.

Pero no bailamos todo el tiempo. Así como papá tenía trabajo que hacer, nosotros teníamos escuela a la cual asistir. Paulette y yo viajamos en autobús una corta distancia a una escuela estadounidense, Escuela Bella Vista. Era una escuela pequeña que ofrecía materias estándar, y practiqué algunos deportes. Mi clase favorita era "Tocar el cuatro".

Augusto asistió a una escuela secundaria católica, San Vicente de Paul, también un corto distancia de casa. Su escuela, junto con la mayoría de las escuelas secundarias venezolanas, requiere la finalización de cinco años de un plan de estudios difícil, con materias sólidas, como física y cálculo y una inmersión obligatoria en un idioma extranjero... Antes de los exámenes finales, los estudiantes venezolanos se quedaban despiertos toda la noche estudiando. Durante esta época, creo que el típico venezolano graduado de secundaria ha probado ser más alfabetizado que el típico graduado universitario estadounidense.

Con una enorme inversión en educación por parte de un gobierno estable, en 1965, aproximadamente el 90% de la población estaba alfabetizada. La universidad pública del Zulia en Maracaibo se convertiría en una de las principales universidades del mundo, ofreciendo títulos profesionales en derecho, medicina, ingeniería. El país estaba produciendo una fuerza de trabajo inteligente y competente para sacar adelante a la nación. No solo las chicas venezolanas eran bonitas y simpáticas. Ellos también eran inteligentes.

A medida que se acercaba el año escolar 1962-63, mis padres decidieron que debería asistir a la Academia Militar de Riverside en Georgia. El amigo de papá, Blackie Armel, que vivía al otro lado de la calle, tenía un hijo, Steve, que estaba en el último año de la escuela de varones. Y así, en septiembre de 1962, entré a la academia. y permanecería allí durante cuatro años de secundaria.

Pero volví a Maracaibo para los veranos. En ese momento, papá había formado una sociedad con Frank Bernard, un colega íntegro y leal de Trinidad. En 1963, incorporaron una nueva empresa llamada "Tri-Can", un proveedor de la industria petrolera local en experiencia de perforación direccional y suministros.

El negocio era bueno para papá y mejoraría. Había estado en el país el tiempo suficiente para establecer contactos confiables y un nombre para sí mismo. El hombre trabajó muy duro, día y noche, y ganó lo que recibió. Nos habíamos mudado una corta distancia a un nuevo rascacielos, al Edificio Yonekura en Bella Vista y Calle 83. El nuevo apartamento era moderno y espacioso, y organicé algunas fiestas de adolescentes allí. Bebimos coca colas y bailamos al ritmo música eterna de Roy Orbison, Bobby Solo y Los Beach Boys.

Durante ese verano conocí a una chica dulce, Irma, quien se convirtió en mi novia. La familia de Irma era de México y su papá trabajaba en Maracaibo. Ella no hablaba inglés en absoluto, y mi español en ese momento era impredecible, así que cada vez que estábamos juntos, teníamos a mano un diccionario español/inglés. Si le preguntara a Irma si le gustaría ir al cine o visitar a un amigo... buscábamos la pregunta, palabra por palabra, y luego ella me corregía la pronunciación. Aunque fastidioso, esta es la forma correcta de aprender un idioma. Agradable inmersión. Su madre también hizo sabrosa comida mexicana desde cero.

Como me uní al equipo de lucha durante mi primer año en Riverside, pensé que entrenar en judo podría ser útil y me mantendría en buena forma. Entonces, me matriculé en una escuela de judo en Maracaibo, impartida por el Sensei Yves Carouget. Sensei Carouget fue el primer maestro en traer judo y aikido a Venezuela, y ostentaba cinturones negros de nivel avanzado en judo, aikido, jiujitsu y también karate. Tuve la suerte de entrenar con él durante tres veranos. En los muchos años transcurridos desde entonces, el Sensei Carouget se ha convertido en una especie de leyenda en los círculos de artes marciales. Me pareció un instructor excelente y duro y un hombre muy agradable.

Una Excursión a Colombia
Durante el verano de 1965, fui con Augusto a Colombia por unas semanas. Para ahorrar dinero, viajábamos en automóvil, autobús y avión. El padre de augusto, Napo, nos condujo tres horas desde Maracaibo hasta Maicao, Colombia, una ciudad cerca de la frontera con Venezuela. Hicimos algunas compras de ropa que podía obtenerse en Maicao por la mitad del precio de artículos similares en Venezuela.

Luego a Villanueva en bus, donde Augusto tenía varios parientes cercanos. Pasamos un día delicioso en la finca de su tío Miguel, llamada "La Victoria", donde montamos a caballo y disfrutamos de una rica parrillada. Villanueva me recordó una escena del viejo oeste americano, donde los vaqueros montaban caballos a la ciudad y los amarraban frente a la tienda de abarrotes. Pero lo más destacado para mí fue conocer a la familia extendida de Augusto. Un tipo de gente como la sal de la tierra. Cada vez que saludaba a un familiar, comenzaba una lluvia de afecto mutuo.

Teníamos la esperanza de tomar un avión en Valledupar que nos llevaría a Bogotá, y así, nos fuimos a Valledupar en bus, un recorrido de 38 millas. Pero los pilotos comerciales colombianos estaban en huelga y no había vuelos disponibles. Nos trasladamos a otro bus y continuamos nuestro camino alegre por 180 millas adicionales hasta Barranquilla.

Aunque estábamos agotados de viajar en autobuses llenos de gente durante casi 250 millas, al llegar a Barranquilla, nos dirigimos al aeropuerto, donde una prima de Augusto, Nancy Ferreira, trabajaba en una línea aérea. "Lo siento, mis amores", nos dijo. "Los pilotos comerciales siguen en paro nacional".

Cansados y sin opciones, tomamos un taxi hasta el centro de Barranquilla. Encontramos un hotel que nos costó $4 por noche. Si buscas la palabra "feo" en el diccionario, debería encontrar una imagen de nuestra habitación de hotel deteriorada. Sucio. Dos camas pequeñas. Colchones con bultos. Sin aire acondicionado.

Encontramos una tienda y compramos una botella grande de aguardiente Cristal de 60 grados, la bebida nacional de Colombia, similar pero más fuerte que el anís francés. Armados con la medicación, entramos en una sala de cine que anunciaba audazmente: "Aire Acondicionado." Y allí nos sentamos, bebiendo aguardiente, amando el aire acondicionado y viendo a John Wayne hablar español.

Al concluir la función doble, tuvimos que abandonar el teatro. Fue por la tarde, y con la caída del sol, la temperatura había bajado un poco. Nuestra habitación de hotel todavía estaba caliente, así que hablábamos un rato, nos duchábamos para refrescarnos, tomar un trago de aguardiente y repetir. Después de tres o cuatro ciclos de este proceso de adormecimiento y enfriamiento, pensamos que podríamos intentar dormir.

Me quedé dormido después de las dos de la madrugada, soñando, estoy seguro, con esquiar en la helada pendiente de una montaña blanca en Alaska. Después de una hora o dos, me despertaron. Algo estaba en mi pierna. Ni idea de qué. Era grande. Subiendo por mi muslo. Tenía muchas piernas. No podía soportar el terror por más tiempo. Saltando de la cama, grité y arrojé a la criatura de mi cuerpo. Encendiendo la luz de la habitación...

ahí estaba en medio del piso... una cucaracha gigante. Un monstruo horrible tan grande como una pelota de béisbol con seis patas. Y ahora, la diabla estaba tratando de escapar. Aproximadamente dos segundos después, el monstruo fue a encontrarse con su creador.

Esa noche no dormimos mucho. A la mañana siguiente, puntualmente al amanecer, nos duchamos y comimos nuestro desayuno. Salimos del Hotel Cucaracha, y cogimos un taxi para que nos llevara al aeropuerto. Afortunadamente, la prima de Augusto estaba de servicio. "Nancy", le preguntamos, "¿hay vuelos comerciales hoy?"
"Lo siento mucho", respondió Nancy, "la huelga continúa".
"¡Pero Nancy, tenemos que ir a Bogotá hoy! Por favor, ¿hay algo?"
"Lo siento", repitió ella. "el único vuelo a Bogotá hoy es un avión de carga".
"Bueno, ¿puedes ponernos en eso?"
"Sería muy incómodo", respondió ella. "No hay asientos".
"No nos importa", dijo Augusto. "Tomaremos cualquier cosa".
"Está bien, entonces", declaró. "Por favor, súbase a la báscula".

Lo cual hicimos. Augusto y yo nos subimos a la báscula y pagamos el pasaje en base a nuestro peso físico. El costo fue de $40 para los dos. Dijimos nuestras gracias y adiós a la encantadora Nancy y abordamos el avión de carga, con nuestro manifiesto de carga pagado en la mano. Una camioneta VW estaba en la nave, y sus puertas estaban abiertas. Así que entramos en el coche, echamos los asientos hacia atrás y pasamos el aguardiente. Volando sobre los Andes fríos, la bebida nos abrigaba, y el avión de hélice saltarín llegó al aeropuerto de Bogotá dos horas después.

La pasamos genial, quedándonos con los abuelos de Augusto en una gran casa en un lindo barrio de Bogotá. Enclavado en los Andes a una altura de 8,600 pies, la ciudad normalmente permanece a unos agradables 65 grados en julio. Asistimos a una corrida de toros, y aprendí la manera de sostener e inclinar una bota para beber vino. Hicimos una visita al extraordinario Museo del Oro, que contiene la mayor colección de oro prehispánico en el mundo. Visitamos un milagro arquitectónico, la Catedral de Sal, proclamada a nivel nacional como "La Primera Maravilla de Colombia". Tuve el honor de sentarme en una silla que perteneció al Gran Libertador, Simón Bolívar.

Fuimos a un bar, repleto, de dos pisos, donde todos cantaban junto con el artista en el escenario. Después de una hora de súplicas, el artista/Maestro de Ceremonias finalmente aceptó una solicitud de mi canción latina favorita...

Todavía puedo escuchar esas 300 voces alzando "Cielito Lindo" hasta los cielos. Finalmente, como agradecimiento justificado a los abuelos de Augusto, les organizamos una serenata a cargo de cantantes folclóricos colombianos. Desafortunadamente, a las 2 AM.

Y luego llegó el momento de que volviéramos a Maracaibo y el momento de que yo volviera a Riverside. Mi último año en la academia militar fue el período más agradable allí, pero estaba extasiado de graduarme el 31 de mayo de 1966. Después de cuatro años de marchar y saludar, iba camino a mi casa en Venezuela.

De vuelta en Maracaibo, retomé los estudios de judo bajo la tutela de Sensei Carouget. Y luego, me invitaron a unirme a una banda de rock. Desde finales de 1966 hasta 1968, tuve el honor de ser el cantante principal de un grupo popular, "Los Hippies".

Nuestra banda de Maracaibo también contó con Carlos Moreno (guitarra principal y cantante), Leopoldo Bohórquez (bajo) y Edgardo Carroz (batería). tocamos música de los Beatles, Rolling Stones y muchos otros. Carlos ("Carlitos") era un guitarrista dotado. Al escuchar una nueva canción por primera vez, la tocaba perfectamente en su primer intento. Algunas de las canciones de nuestro repertorio incluyen: "As Tears Go By" (Stones), "Good Lovin'" (Rascals), "It Won't Be Long" (Beatles), "House of the Rising Sun" (Animals), "Like A Rolling Stone" (Dylan) y "Love Potion #9" (Searchers).

Nuestro manager, León, nos reservó para tocar en la mayoría de los lugares populares de la ciudad, incluyendo Club Bella Vista, Club Alianza, Club Náutico y Club Comercio. Hicimos un poco de dinero y nos divertimos mucho tocando para el público adolescente. La música de finales de los sesenta fue una fusión de introversión y extroversión, y los artistas comunicaban sus pensamientos y sentimientos más íntimos, poéticamente, a través de la música melódica. La juventud venezolana de la época sabía algo estaba pasando, y querían ser parte de ello.

Recuerdo una noche especial con Los Hippies. Nuestro gerente, León, había reservado dos conciertos para la banda esa noche, a unas cuatro millas de distancia. Tocaríamos seis canciones en el Club Bella Vista, luego correríamos a la camioneta Ford con guitarras y palillos de tambor en la mano. Los años sesenta se esfumaron para Los Hippies, en parte debido a la conducción de León.

León nos llevó al segundo espectáculo, la celebración de Quince años de una joven, donde esperaba otro juego de amplificadores Fender. Después de que salimos del auto como The Monkees, Carlitos se conectó y atacó el ritmo de apertura del rockero, "Roll Over Beethoven." Mientras cantábamos... *Gonna write a little letter / Gonna mail it to my local DJ...* esos alegres maracuchos bailaron como si su vida dependiera de ello.

Después de que terminaban las fiestas, tarde en la noche, Augusto y yo íbamos al norte a las afueras de Maracaibo a Puerto Caballo, un modesto restaurante en el lago. Servían pescado fresco del día. Pediríamos bagre entero a la brasa, con yuca por 2 Bs. (47 centavos de dólar estadounidense). Aprecio ese recuerdo... Sopla una brisa fresca. Una luna plateada reflejándose en el agua cristalina. Una deliciosa comida con buenos amigos, Jorge Hernández y Germán Parra.

El ejército de los EE. UU. me enlazó en enero de 1968, y me ordenaron reportarme a la oficina de reclutamiento en América. Serví mi tiempo en el ejército y después, la vida me llevó en varias direcciones diferentes. Desde entonces, durante estos muchos años, he regresado a Maracaibo varias veces. Aunque soy un nativo californiano, no dejé mi corazón en San Francisco. Cuando cierro mis ojos cansados y viejos ... mi corazón regresa a la Venezuela que fue.

Oh señor, la Venezuela que fue. Un gobierno estable. Una economía estable. Un país haciendo mejoras en infraestructura. Gente altamente educada. Calles sumamente seguras. Transporte publico económico. Comida barata y deliciosa. Una clase media amplia y con futuro sólido.

La Venezuela que es
Desde que mi familia dejó Venezuela, ¿qué ha cambiado?

Todo. En un esfuerzo por controlar su destino controlando completamente su recurso más valioso, la industria petrolera del país fue nacionalizada en 1976. Mientras que la idea de la industria petrolera propiedad del Estado, independiente de la influencia extranjera, comenzó como una manera de controlar el destino del país, irónicamente, terminó como el comienzo de su caída. La nacionalización como concepto es convincente, pero la pérdida de asistencia técnica de Estados Unidos, Alemania y los Países Bajos han demostrado ser catastróficos.

Lamentablemente, la vida en Venezuela hoy se ha deteriorado al borde del colapso cercano, principalmente debido a dos pilotos de kamikaze: Hugo Chávez y Nicolás Maduro. Sirviendo como presidente de Venezuela desde 1999-2013, Chávez se alineó con los gobiernos marxistas-leninistas de Fidel y luego Raúl Castro en Cuba. Siendo un destacado adversario de los Estados Unidos, Chávez describió sus Políticas como antiimperialistas.

Debido a la muerte de Chávez en 2013, el vicepresidente Nicolás Maduro asumió la presidencia, y él permanece en esa posición hoy. Durante el reinado de Maduro, según la Unión Nacional de Trabajadores de la Prensa de Venezuela, 115 puntos de venta de periódicos se han cerrado. Y desde 2019, Venezuela ha sido expuesta a "apagones de información" frecuentes, períodos sin acceso a Internet o a servicios de noticias durante eventos políticos importantes. ¿Qué se esconde Maduro?

Todo. El empleo se ha desplomado. Los salarios son una fracción de lo que fueron, y según la BBC, tres de cuatro venezolanos viven en extrema pobreza. Los precios se han disparado ... para 2019, el Banco Mundial estimó la inflación en 10 millones por ciento! Los cajeros automáticos están vacíos. Las estaciones de servicio están vacías. La investigación realizada por Caritas muestra que el 70% de los niños muestran signos de desnutrición. Y según la revista *New Yorker*, Venezuela tiene lo más alta tasa de criminalidad violenta del mundo ... incluso las escaleras en un hospital público no están a salvo de ladrones, que se aprovechan del personal y los pacientes.

Según lo documentado por las Naciones Unidas, bajo el gobierno de Maduro, más de 9.000 personas han sido objeto de ejecuciones extrajudiciales, y casi 6 millones de venezolanos se han visto obligados a huir del país. Incluido en la larga lista de refugiados políticos es la hija mayor de Augusto, Alexandra, quien con de manera segura escapó a los Estados Unidos con su familia en abril de 2015.

Los crímenes de Maduro contra todos y contra todo continúan. En 2020, el Departamento de Justicia de Estados Unidos lo acusó de cargos de narcotráfico y narcoterrorismo, y el Departamento de Estado de EE. UU. ha ofrecido una recompensa de $15 millones para obtener información que ayude a llevar al criminal ante la justicia. ¿Quién apoya a Maduro? Rusia, China, Irán, Siria y Cuba.

¿Qué pasa con el hermoso lago de Maracaibo? El biólogo local Alejandro Álvarez dijo: "Es como vivir al lado de un inodoro. Nada bueno puede salir de eso". Oliendo a refinería de petróleo, la vasta extensión del lago de Maracaibo se ha vuelto altamente contaminada por sus reservas de crudo, ya que el colapso económico de Venezuela dejó pozos y oleoductos en ruinas.

¿Cómo pudo pasar esto? Un informe revelador de Transparencia Internacional: Venezuela ocupa el puesto 176 entre 180 países en su Índice de Corrupción 2021. Maduro y sus compinches, prófugos de la justicia, a salvo en el palacio presidencial bajo la protección de las fuerzas de seguridad cubanas de élite, siguen disfrutando de caviar ruso y puros cubanos... mientras el pueblo muere.

Anteriormente en este artículo, se hizo referencia a Chávez y Maduro como pilotos kamikazes. Eso no es exactamente correcto. Matan todo menos a ellos mismos.

Mi corazón está con mis hermanos y hermanas venezolanos.

Mis palabras finales son para el Sr. Maduro y sus seguidores dispuestos:

Crímenes contra la humanidad.
Delitos contra la naturaleza.
Crímenes contra Dios.

~~~~~

ABOUT THE ILLUSTRATOR

Brandon Olterman was raised by a hard-working family in the verdant beauty of southern Ohio. He was interested in drawing from the time he could hold a green marker, one imprinted with the words, *Camden Fence Company*. That would be his dad's company and has been the family's primary line of work for five generations. Along with his younger brothers, Ryan and Tanner, Brandon assisted his dad by building fences before going to college.

Brandon attended Bluffton University on a soccer scholarship, and graduated with a bachelor's degree in Fine Art and Graphic Design. During college, he served as cartoonist for the school paper, *The Witmarsum*, where his main focus was on comic illustrations. Every day he would draw at least one strip to train himself to become a working cartoonist. By the time school was over, however, Brandon no longer wanted to illustrate cartoons.

So, he redirected his skillset elsewhere. Brandon moved to sunny California and easily fell into the art of commercial screen-printing. During this time, he illustrated his first children's book, Kates's First Mate. Brandon then moved to an artist colony in downtown Los Angeles, called the *Think Tank*. Here, he learned the ins and outs of running a gallery and putting on art shows.

A few years later, Brandon married Megan Kashi Ziemer. They have one son, Felix, and together they travel the country. Megan is a traveling, registered nurse, and she saves lives daily, while Brandon takes care of the household and creates art.

Brandon is currently producing his own series of books called The Nutshell, which features his cartoons, poetry and short stories. He dabbles in the design of board and card games, and additionally, Brandon is working on another children's book and a coloring book.

Joe Ziemer is very grateful to Brandon for creating his insightful illustrations exclusively for Wavelengths.

Brandon's artwork appears on the front and back cover and on pages 8, 26, 48, 56, 64, 66, 68, 78, 82, 94 and 108.

ABOUT THE AUTHOR

Following the Second World War, Joe Ziemer's parents left Oklahoma for the sandy pastures of southern California. Born in 1948, Joe spent his early years in Bakersfield, a tough oil town. When he turned 12, the family moved south to an even tougher oil town... to Maracaibo, Venezuela... where Joe and his sister Paulette felt like they were the only blondes in the country.

Five years later, Joe graduated from Riverside Military Academy in Georgia as Superior Cadet. He then joined Los Hippies, a rock band in Maracaibo. The group performed early Stones and Beatles music, so much fun to play, plus it was an ideal way to meet girls. The U.S. Army lassoed Joe in 1968, assigning him to the top-secret Courier Service in Washington D.C.

After completing his military obligation during the turbulent Vietnam war era, Joe enrolled in College of the Redwoods (CR), where he was honored to serve as Student Body President. Joe remains grateful to CR's brilliant English professor, Mrs. Barbara Wrede, for her unshakable encouragement. Additional studies at the University of California at Davis brought a B.A. in Social Psychology and appointment as a Regents Scholar.

Joe has assisted worldwide broadcasters for 40 years, supplying transmission systems to radio and TV stations. In 1996, his Indiana firm won a prestigious Exporter of the Year award. The job has taken him to over 100 countries, and from his travels, Joe says he sees no difference between extreme left and extreme right governments. In both cases, the people suffer terribly.

Actively passionate about free speech, Joe served as Editor of *Radio World International* newspaper for five years. He has written several journal articles, and after years of study, Joe authored the acclaimed biography on his friend, Mickey Newbury - Crystal & Stone, first and second editions.

Joe is happily married to Roxanne (married way over his head) and is very proud to be the father of five children: Donovan, Jamie, Kris, Joey and Megan. Furthermore, Joe is especially blessed to have seven delightful grandchildren: Warren, Aaron, Trustin, Honor, Felix, Lola and Alice.

~~~~~

It's a wavelength thing
Who and what one hears while here
Be sharp or be flat